OPHESY

JUST DO IT!

PROPHESY
JUST DO IT!

MATT HELLAND

ARROWZ

Prophesy—Just Do It!

Copyright © 2019 Matthew Helland

Published by Arrowz Publishing House
info@arrowz.org
www.arrowz.org

Author: Matthew Helland
Editor: Erica Kramer
Art direction and interior design: Ronald Gabrielsen, 3ig.com

ISBN 978 94 90489 52 6

I dedicate this book to my wife, Femke.

*Everything that is truly valuable was given to me
by Jesus and by you. You're the greatest gift
I have ever received, and through you and
through Jesus I have become who I am today.*

❧

Pursue love, and earnestly desire the spiritual gifts,
especially that you may prophesy.

– 1 CORINTHIANS 14:1

For you can all prophesy one by one,
so that all may learn and all be encouraged.

– 1 CORINTHIANS 14:31

Contents

Endorsements 9

Foreword 11

Introduction: The Power of Prophecy 13

The Vision: The Return of the Prophets 21

1. Hearing God's Voice 25
2. Keys 43
3. Barriers 73
4. Prophecy in the Church 99
5. Teaching Children to Prophesy 121

Conclusion: Creating a Healthy Prophetic Culture ... 131

Notes 136

Recommended Reading 137

About the Author 138

Endorsements

Matthew Helland is the type of guy that brings the refreshing love of God wherever he goes. If you have the opportunity to meet him I wholeheartedly recommend him concerning all ministry.

– *Phil Strout*
National Director of Vineyard Association of Churches, USA

Lives are changed once we begin to recognize and activate the power of the Holy Spirit in every believer. I am amazed at how Matthew's knowledge and practical teachings have ignited the supernatural in our region.

– *Mark Hammond*
Senior Pastor of Celebration Center IPHC, Modesto, CA, USA

Matthew Helland has organized schools of prophecy around the world. He is a reliable, humble and dedicated servant of God whose integrity is beyond reproach. For that reason, I wholeheartedly recommend this book!

– *Jan Pool*
Founder and Senior Leader of Heartlink, the Netherlands

This is a book for every believer to read and enjoy.

– *Randell O. Drake*

Bishop of New Horizons Ministries, I.P.H.C.

Matthew Helland has dared to write a book that is biblical, contemporary, practical and autobiographical. I am pleased to recommend it.

– *Thomson Mathew*

Professor and Former Dean, College of Theology & Ministry, Oral Roberts University, Tulsa, OK, USA

Matthew Helland will inspire you to expect to see Jesus do more than you knew was possible. This book will give you practical teaching, helpful tools, and stories that will spark you to step out and see amazing things!

– *Putty Putman*

Founding Director of School of Kingdom Ministry, Pastor at The Vineyard of Central Illinois, Urbana, IL, USA

Foreword

Over the years I have been blessed by words of encouragement and prophetic insight Matthew has given to me. When I see a message from Matt, I know I am hearing from a man who has spent time with God, a man who genuinely loves me and seeks the best for me, a man who has sought to determine God's timing in what, and how, he should speak.

This book is part autobiography and part instruction. It is a lesson in Holy Spirit gifts, in taking the time to develop those gifts, and then giving God glory for the effective deployment of those gifts.

I've read a lot of books about prophetic ministry, but this one is different. It is written from the front lines of confronting the desperate needs of people in Western culture, specifically Western Europe.

Matt is giving his life to raising up new a generation dedicated to the One who is "the Way, the Truth, and the Life." They are open to the fullness of His Spirit. They understand He is the Redeemer. They understand He is Love. They know that He is Truth. And they know, that He is seeking to reveal Himself to all who are thirsty in a modern spiritual desert.

What makes this book so appealing is Matt Helland's willingness to be "real." He shares his fears, lack of knowledge (and how to address it), and even his failures in exercising spiritual gifts. There is a joyful humility that runs through this book. However, this humility does not mask the genuine courage it takes to reach people. As you read this book, you will be inspired, informed. And more: I believe an impartation will take place.

Prophesy—Just Do It is a must-read book for living out the fullness of the Spirit in our generation.

– Dr. A.D. Beacham, Jr.
Bishop of the International Pentecostal Holiness Church

The Power of Prophecy

Every week, my wife and I visit Spanish-speaking workers in Amsterdam's Red-light District. There, I am known as Pastor or Padre Mateo, who comes by to listen to and to pray for everyone who opens their door to him. On a regular basis I see people receiving physical healing or being touched by an accurate word from God I share with them. Their stories show how God's love has transformed lives through prophecy.

One woman I will call Victoria told me about the first time she met me. She thought I was a potential client so she was shocked when she opened the door and I began giving her an accurate word from God. She had been on her knees asking God for a word from him, and in walked Pastor Mateo answering the question she had asked God that morning in prayer. In addition, all the pain in her back disappeared after I prayed for her.

Another woman in the room had just had a dream and asked me if I could tell her what it meant. She burst into tears as I described what she was going through. Victoria told me the woman immediately went upstairs, put her clothes on and never returned to working in the Red-light District.

One of the first women we were able to help get out of prostitution, Maria, always sat with her feet against the window in a peculiar fashion. Later I learned this was because of severe knee and back pain she was suffering. She never talked to me and later I found out she had told everyone I was a crazy white man who spoke Spanish and told everybody he was a pastor. One of her colleagues told her I really was a pastor and I could really help her.

I was excited when Maria told me she wanted to quit prostitution and wanted our help. Later that week, when she arrived at the office of Bright Fame, she told me she was afraid of "becoming one of those Christians." To this I just responded, "Oh, don't worry about it at all."

We helped Maria quit her work in the Red-light District and every time I saw her I prayed for the healing of her knee and back. Again, she politely allowed me to pray for her. She later told me she thought, "This man is crazy."

One day we had a barbecue at her house and I had invited a prophetic friend of mine. The first thing he said when he saw her was, "I see your knee is bone on bone, without cartilage. God is going to heal your knee and your back." Maria thought he was crazy and responded, "I would really like to quit drinking." My friend responded, "Okay, the next time you drink alcohol, you will feel terrible." That day she had some beer, but it just did not taste like it used to. The next morning, she woke up and she had a major hangover something she never had as she was used to drinking large amounts of whisky, wine and beer. Alcohol had been one of her coping mechanisms, but since that day, she hasn't needed it.

Maria's life has radically changed since she has gotten to know Christ. She has quit drinking, her nightmares have stopped, she has lost weight, her body has healed and she has regained joy in life. She has also learned how to ride a bike and swim, two important skills for anyone living in Holland.

Maria worked in prostitution for over sixteen years, but now she has a totally new life. The woman who had said she was afraid of becoming a Christian now has Bible study at her house every Tuesday evening. Every week new people are attending and getting to know Christ through Maria's cooking and testimony. She is a key figure in a new church in Amsterdam called Iglesia Vida Nueva, or New Life Church.

All around the world, prophecy changes lives. In June of 2018, I visited the Red-light District of Mexicali, Mexico together with a team of young Christians. We had asked God for clues or words of knowledge concerning the people we would find that day. One of the words was "camouflage." One of the young evangelists saw a man with a camouflage shirt and ran after him. He was shocked to see the wearer had been his cellmate in jail for over a year and a half. His old friend looked at him and said, "For the last three days, I have been asking God to send someone to me to tell me about Him and help me start a new life." As my friend began praying for him, his old cellmate fell into his arms and began to weep.

This young man learned that evangelism and prophecy are not difficult at all. They are simply all about communicating the heart and mind of Christ to the world around us. From Amsterdam to Budapest, and from Kiev to Barcelona and Mexicali, I have seen people being moved to tears because someone told them about God's heart for them. At times this may be accompanied with a healing or an accurate word of knowledge, but the most important goal is to communicate God's truth and love for them.

Every person I train in prophetic ministry will at some point in their message utter such a word as, "God says, 'I love you,'" or "You are my beloved child." Evangelism and prophetic ministry are all about sharing love, truth, hope and life. In this book, I will focus on the often misunderstood and feared ministry of prophecy.

What is Prophecy?

Prophecy is communicating the heart and mind of God to your world. It is knowing God's voice so well it becomes normal to tell others what we feel God wants to tell them. Prophecy transforms lives and releases the power of God into our world. Proverbs 29:18 says without prophetic vision or without prophecy the people of God perish. In other words, the Church begins to die when we only know *about* God and we don't really know *Him*. Prophecy is the natural fruit of cultivating a personal interactive relationship with God.

If He is our Father and we are His children it should be the most natural thing to hear His voice and communicate His words to others. Prophecy should be normal among Christians.

Why Prophesy?

Firstly, because the Bible tells us to on numerous occasions. The apostle Peter says if anyone speaks, they should speak as if they were speaking "the very words of God" (1 Pet. 4:11 NIV). He also states on the day of Pentecost that in the last days God would pour out His Spirit on all flesh and everyone would prophesy (see Act. 2:17-18). The apostle Paul explicitly states to "follow the way of love and eagerly desire gifts of the Spirit, especially prophecy" (1 Cor. 14:1 NIV). And these are just a few of the scriptures urging us to prophesy and flow in the gifts of the Holy Spirit.

Secondly, because hearing God's voice is a regular part of following Jesus (see John 10:3-5). Jesus is the good Shepherd and we are His sheep. We follow Him because He calls us by name and we recognize His voice. He does not drive us with fear or manipulation but goes ahead of us and calls us by name. In the same way I recognize my wife or my mother's voice on the telephone when they call, anyone who believes in Christ can hear him and get to know God's voice.

And finally, because it reveals God's heart, what could be better?

Near the end of a youth prophetic conference I led in Budapest, a young man grabbed the microphone and said, "God says, 'I love you, I love you, I love you.'" I did not brush this off as too elemental. Instead, I thought, "Yes! He caught the essence of the prophetic ministry." It revealed the passionate, loving heart and mind of Father God. He longs for His children to know Him as He truly is. He loves to speak to and through us.

Embracing Transformation

Unfortunately, prophecy is not always present in the local church today, partly because of a lack of knowledge or healthy role models who can demonstrate and explain the proper use of the gifts of the Spirit. Relatively few people are willing to teach and activate other people in prophecy. Many people would like to prophesy, but they just don't know how or are frightened by incorrect teaching.

This is why I wrote this book. I'm not a know-it-all expert, but as a fellow mountain climber who delights in helping others climb higher, I have learned growing in prophetic ministry is best done in the context of community. I gladly share my successes and failures; I believe they will encourage you to grow in your ability to hear God's voice and move in His power.

I have seen churches transformed after organizing a school of prophecy. Like those schools, this book is meant to equip you to prophesy. It is full of biblical examples and modern-day stories to inspire you. I have been privileged to teach this material in cities all across the world and have seen wonderful results. Adults and children who thought they could never prophesy are now confidently and accurately prophesying.

The biblical principles I share will help you if you long to grow in prophetic ministry. But at its core, the prophetic ministry is not about principles or steps. It is all about developing your intimate relationship with God. When we live connected to Jesus, all the gifts of the Spirit, including prophecy, can be normal and natural. If we seek His presence first—His presents follow.

My attitude regarding prophetic ministry is, "Everything I can do, you can do better." That motto was inspired by Jesus' words, "Very truly I tell you, whoever believes in me will do the works I have been doing, and they will do even greater things than these, because I am going to the Father" (John 14:12 NIV). Pause for a moment to take that in: Jesus Himself said we would do the same works He did—and even greater. He left us His Holy Spirit to empower us to do these things.

The prophet Ezekiel shares a vision. A river coming out of God's temple becomes so deep he can swim in it. Everywhere the river goes, new life appears and things flourish (Ez. 47). What a great description of what can happen as people grow in life-giving and biblical prophetic ministry. It is like being able to swim in the flow of the Holy Spirit. Yet, the hardest part of that kind of swimming is getting started. It's like getting into the cold water of a mountain lake or the

Dutch sea. I remember one time standing in the water for ten minutes before I dared dive into the chilly waves. Once I dived in, however, I enjoyed swimming and my body got used to the temperature.

Of all our family, there is one person who loves to dive into water no matter how cold it is: Benjamin, my now six-year-old son. Cold water does not stop him from diving into the waves of the North Sea. He has such fun swimming, no matter how cold it may be. It's the same with prophecy; once you jump in, you will discover how much fun it is! The courage Benjamin has to jump in cold water is the courage I want to have to prophesy over people, no matter how frigid a response I get.

Surfers and divers who swim in cold waters use wet suits so they can swim no matter how cold the water may be. I pray this book with all of the biblical principles, examples and exercises will allow you to swim in the flow of what the Holy Spirit is doing and saying.

It is my hope you will enjoy reading this book, but even more so I my desire is that you further cultivate your own intimate relationship with Jesus and learn to prophesy! Learn to see how God can change your life and the lives of people around you when you humbly yet boldly speak His words and move in the power of His Holy Spirit.

The Return of the Prophets

Pray for the rising up of a new generation of leaders—prophets of the apostolic mold—leaders who could once again gather the people of God into communities of radical faithfulness.
– RICHARD FOSTER[1]

In 1978, Christian author and theologian Richard Foster was strolling across a beach in Portland, Oregon. All of a sudden, God started to talk to him. During that conversation, he noticed a large rock in the middle of the water being beaten by waves. It stood as a bastion of unconquerable strength. Then he saw an ancient tree which had been hit by lightning. The tree was dead in the middle and only had a few parts on the outside which were still alive. As he looked, God said to him "the Church in many places looks like the ancient tree: dead in the middle with only small remnants of life on the periphery." He turned again and looked at the strong rock beaten by the waves and heard God say, "But that rock is what I am calling my Church to be like."

Foster writes, "I was given ... guidance to pray for the rising up of a new generation of leaders—prophets of the apostolic mold.

Leaders who could once again gather the people of God into communities of radical faithfulness."

He goes on to describe these prophets by saying,

> They come from every class and category of people. Some are educated; others are illiterate or semi-literate. Some come from organized churches and denominations; others come from outside these structures. Some are women; some are men; some are children. To the person they love Jesus with their whole heart. Under their leadership and by the power of the Holy Spirit the people of God are once again being gathered. (I am speaking not organizationally but organically.) We are witnessing in our day a whole host of children and women and men who are getting hooked into a different order of reality and power.[2]

Foster's vision strikes a chord in me. In it, I see my own desire to be a prophet of the apostolic mold who will gather God's people into communities of radical faithfulness. They align with my mission to reach the lost, make disciples, raise up a new generation of prophets, and create life-changing communities where knowing God and hearing from Him is normal.

Many Christians do not believe it is possible to hear God's voice or see visions from Him. But I am convinced God created us to be able to hear His voice. God still speaks today. The problem is all too often we are not listening, either due to unbelief or poor spiritual leadership. Sometimes, the leaders of our communities lack the knowledge and skills to develop a dynamic relationship with God. The Bible teaches us God raises up prophets when people do not know Him. In 1 Samuel, we read an example: "But when they arrived and saw Samuel leading a group of prophets who were prophesying, the Spirit of God came upon Saul's men, and they also began to prophesy" (1 Sam. 19:20 NLT)." In 2 Kings 2, we find large communities of prophets in places such as Gilgal, Bethel and Jericho. The norm was not one or two individuals prophesied, but entire communities.

I am convinced it is God's intention not to just raise up an individual prophet, but communities of prophets who regularly prophesy and can activate others to learn to recognize God's voice for themselves and others.

In fact, it is not God's will for just one or two "special" people to be able to prophesy, but that all may prophesy. Paul writes, "For you can *all* prophesy in turn so that everyone may be instructed and encouraged" (1 Cor. 14:31 NIV). And in Acts we read, "In the last days, God says, I will pour out my Spirit on *all* people. Your sons and daughters will prophesy, your young men will see visions, your old men will dream dreams. Even on my servants, both men and women, I will pour out my Spirit in those days, and they will prophesy" (Act. 2:17-18 NIV).

Here we see the promise is for all people—male, female, young, old, rich, poor —everyone upon whom God pours out His Spirit. The new covenant God made with His people was that everyone could know God and speak His words (see Jer. 31:33-34).

In some Church traditions, only the church leaders can receive and give a message from God. Not only is this unbiblical, it is a tragedy people are made dependent on one or two leaders if they want to communicate with God. It is unhealthy if a believer relies too heavily on a prophet, counselor, pastor or leader in order to get direction from God for their lives. We can each learn to be led by the Holy Spirit and the Bible. We should not start by looking to prophets for direction in our lives. We look to God first and only then to other people who know Him and will confirm what He speaks to our own hearts.

It is not only special "prophets" or ministers who get to prophesy. Often, it is my favorite prophetic ministers: my own children or people nobody else would suspect of being able to prophesy. When I release Bible school students to do prophetic and healing ministry, they normally begin seeing the same kinds of healings and prophetic ministry I minister with. God wants every believer to be able to prophesy!

So, would you like to be a part of a new generation of prophets? Would you like to learn how prophesying can be normal and natural for you? Let's start at the beginning, then: how to hear God's voice.

CHAPTER 1

Hearing God's Voice

I will instruct you and teach you in the way you should go;
I will counsel you with my eye upon you.
– PSALM 32:8

There is life-changing power in hearing God's voice. This is what Dutchman Piet van Soest can testify to. As a twelve-year-old boy, he told everyone someday he would have a chocolate store. However, at the age of fifty-two, health problems made it nearly impossible for him to walk. Walking is essential for work in a bakery, so doctors wanted to put him on disability benefits. They did not believe he would ever be able to work again. He remembered, though, that God had told him years earlier he would have a chocolate store.

By faith, he began renting a small shop in the town of Hillegom when a miracle took place. He was completely healed. After he learned how to make chocolate from different chocolatiers, his only problem was he did not have a recipe for making chocolate bonbons. One night, he asked God for it and went to sleep. The next day he woke up with a recipe in his thoughts. God gave him a dream from which he made his first bonbons out of chocolate, caramel and whipped cream.

This process of getting a recipe repeated itself five times. His chocolate store is now known for its special recipes. When someone asks him how he gets them, he replies, "I get them from God in a dream." To this day, you can taste these delicious chocolates at Chocolaterie Pierre in Hillegom and Haarlem, Holland. Even now, his best sellers are the bonbons made from the recipe he received from God

This same power is visible in the life of Frits Rouvoet, founder and director of Bright Fame. Frits was in a meeting in the United States when a prophet picked him out. He began describing the building and the kind of ministry he would be doing in downtown Amsterdam. Later, Frits started working in a building in the city center. After a few days he realized this was the building the prophet had described. The prophet had also said, "If you start working there, the Mary Magdalenes will come in." Not long afterward the women of the Red-light District started coming in for help.

His work developed into a ministry that stops human trafficking and has helped hundreds of women get out of prostitution. My wife, Femke, and I are privileged to be a part of this organization. To this day, that prophetic word is having an effect on not only Rouvoet's life, but on the lives of many others.

But how can we hear God's voice? That's what I once asked a prophet: "How can I prophesy?" He looked at me and said, "The same Holy Spirit I have, you have too. Just do it!" I believed him, and that was the beginning of me regularly prophesying and using the gifts of the Holy Spirit. "So, does

God always speak to you?" someone once asked me. I replied, "Yes, but the problem is I am not always listening." This is true for many of us: God is always speaking, but how often are we really listening?

God speaks to us in many different ways: through Scripture, pictures, nature, circumstances, good advice, dreams, the church, common sense, our desires and more. The difficult bit is not so much hearing God's voice but recognizing when He is speaking to us. Everyone who wants to grow in hearing God's voice has to learn how to differentiate between what God is saying, what comes from our own heart and what the enemy is saying.

If we want to hear and discern God's voice, it's important we know the Bible. God's primary modus operandi for speaking to us and warming our hearts is through the Bible. That is the standard by which all gifts and prophetic words from God should be judged.

God Speaks Through the Bible

> My son, be attentive to my words; incline your ear to my sayings.
> – PROVERBS 4:20

God often speaks to us and those around us through Scripture. Amazing things start to happen when we listen to God's voice and apply His Word to our lives and to those around us. God often highlights passages to us: things we just need to hear right now. We may be reminded of a Bible verse when we need to act or when we need to stop doing something. This is not our brain telling us things, it can be God speaking to us through his Word.

I have a fun area of ministry that has produced amazing results. I like to minister at psychic fairs. I bring about forty to fifty Scripture cards which I put printed face down on my table. I am continually amazed at how often God speaks to people directly when they randomly pick a Scripture card. The Bible always serves as a diving board from which I can speak into people's lives.

One little girl came to my table and told me she wanted to know her future. I told her to pick a card and she randomly got Jeremiah 29:11: "For I know the plans I have for you, declares the LORD, plans for welfare and not for evil, to give you a future and a hope." I told her, "See, God knows your future and He wants you to get to know Him through Jesus." I then got to pray with her and her mother and they invited Jesus to come into their lives that day.

A man interviewed me for a radio program and asked me to tell him his future. Again, I told him to pick a card. "I will be a father to you, and you shall be sons and daughters to me, says the LORD Almighty" (2 Cor. 6:18). This scripture along with some accurate information God gave me about his life gave me a wonderful opportunity to share the gospel with him. The Word of God is living and active, and when people begin to believe it and apply it to their lives, amazing things can happen (see Heb. 4:12).

God speaks to me every day when I meditate, pray and read the Bible. I can speak into people's lives with so much more authority and confidence when I speak Scripture over them. This can be as simple as saying something like this: "The Lord says I am your Shepherd and I will take care of you. I love you with an everlasting love. I want you to be of good courage because I will never leave you nor forsake you. Do not fear and do not worry for I am with you and I will care for you. As the heavens are higher than the earth, so great is my love for you" (see Matt. 6:34; Deut. 31:6; Ps. 23:1, 103:11; Jer: 31:3).

Do not underestimate how powerful a scripture or a Bible story can be to impact someone's life. I fill myself up with Scripture so when I pray for someone the Holy Spirit can direct my prayer. Then I pray exactly what they need to hear (see John 14:26). There was a time in my life when I struggled with depression through culture shock. Meditating on Scripture was a powerful antidote for the hopelessness I felt. Something that really helped was to make a list of all the things I am because of Christ. Every day I would read this list aloud and my identity started shifting from how I felt to who God says I am.

One of my relatives told me the only way she survived dark emotional times in her life was to get away, study her Bible and pray. This is what enabled her to come out victorious.

Confessing Scripture over our lives by praying and meditating on it is a proven way to change our lives from the inside out. It helps us to get God's perspective about our lives.

We cannot base our life choices on our emotions. If life was led by emotions, it would be like a roller coaster going up and down depending on our circumstances (see Eph. 4:14). We must anchor our identity in the Word of God, because it does not change (see Matt. 24:35). It is as applicable today as it was the day God inspired someone to write it.

We should tend to our hearts as a gardener tends to their garden. We must fill our hearts with the Bible so God's word can produce beautiful flowers and fruit such as joy, peace, love and patience (see Gal. 5:22-23).

When we pull the weeds of bitterness, unforgiveness and pain out of our hearts, we create a safe place where we can walk daily with Jesus and listen to His voice. Reading and applying Scripture to our life can bring true life change. It is the solid rock foundation upon which we can build our life.

The Bible, then, is God's mouthpiece. It is the anchor of our identity and the touchstone by which we test every prophetic word. All prophetic words *must* submit to Scripture. God is not schizophrenic: He will not tell someone to lie, cheat, gossip, murder, hate, or commit adultery. His Word speaks so clearly against these things. So, Scripture is what we use to prophesy and to evaluate all prophecy.

God Speaks Through Pictures

> Hear my words: If there is a prophet among you, I the LORD make myself known to him in a vision; I speak with him in a dream.
> – NUMBERS 12:6

The Bible is full of examples of God speaking to people through dreams and visions which at first glance may not necessarily make much sense. God loves to speak to us through pictures and symbols. He spoke to Abraham using the stars of the sky and the grains of sand of the seashore (see Gen. 15:5, 22:17). God is continually speaking to us through nature and things in our surroundings (see Ps. 19). Just like a picture is worth a thousand words, so a dream or a vision can be worth a million words.

Jesus Himself was the master storyteller. He was always telling stories and parables with multiple meanings. Imagine if you were sitting across from Jesus at a dinner table. He grabs the saltshaker and says, "You are the salt of the earth" (see Matt. 5:13). Or He points at birds outside and says: "The Father takes care of them" (see Matt. 6:26). God has not stopped speaking to us through stories and pictures.

An easy and common way God shows us a picture is through our imagination. If I were to say, "Imagine a pink elephant ice skating in a purple dress," you can probably see that in your mind's eye. I have learned God often gives me a picture that has a relevant meaning for someone. Prophecy is unpacking that picture and explaining what God wants to say through it.

What makes pictures difficult is you don't always know what is literal and what is symbolic. One day, I told a man I saw him working on an oilrig. I figured it was symbolic. He then told me he literally worked on an oilrig. Another time I told a woman God wanted her to dance. I again figured it was symbolic. What I did not know was she had just quit dancing because she felt she was not good enough.

On the other hand, I was once at a church when I saw a picture of a pancake that needed to be flipped. After the service, I realized God used the same imagery when he called Ephraim to change (see Hos. 7:8). The church did not have a literal pancake to flip, nor was God calling them to open a pancake restaurant. The church was facing an important season of transition and change. The picture confirmed their belief that change was needed. Interpreting prophetic pictures is fun, but also tricky. Part of growing in prophetic ministry is learning how to discern what God is saying to someone literally or symbolically.

The more you prophesy, the more you will develop a special "sign language" with God. For example, many times when I feel God is highlighting someone's nose, He is speaking of a gift of discernment. Their mouth is about a gift of speaking. The ears mean they are good listeners. If their knees are highlighted, God is talking about their prayer life. The more I prophesy, the more I experience certain symbols God uses to speak to me – symbols which often have a similar meaning. God will speak to you in a unique way so you will understand Him.

The prophet Wim Kok from Bunschoten works at a machine shop. It is normal for him to give me a prophetic word describing tools and machinery he works with all day. Jesus spoke to fishermen about fishing and farmers about farming. Peter was hungry when he saw an image of animals he was to slaughter and eat (see Acts 10:13).

For those who are dog lovers, God may use a picture of a dog which would mean faithfulness, companionship and love. For someone who is afraid of dogs, this may mean something fearful or negative. What may mean one thing in one context to one person may mean something totally different to another. This is why it is good to be dependent on the leading of the Holy Spirit when we interpret dreams and pictures.

God Speaks Through Our Feelings and Desires

Keep them [God's words] within your heart.
– PROVERBS 4:21b

God often speaks through impulses, feelings and desires. For example, as a teenager, I suddenly felt I had to visit my workplace on a Friday night to talk to my colleague. When I arrived, I told her, "God says it does not matter what kind of mess you are in in, He wants to help you out." She replied,

"Boy, am I in a big mess!" The next day I found out she had been in the process of stealing thousands of dollars from our employer that very night.

On another day, I felt like I had to call a good friend of mine in Bolivia who I had not spoken to in over three years. My phone call lasted about sixty seconds, and in that conversation I told him, "God wants you to start a new church." He had just asked God whether or not he should start a new church. The church that came out of this is doing very well.[3]

When ministering prophetically, I often feel drawn to people like an invisible string pulling me in their direction. I know then that I need to say or do something for this person. It is also not uncommon for me to send friends on Facebook an encouraging message on impulse. Sometimes I will get a response saying something like, "How did you know you had to send me this? God gave me the same scripture yesterday in my time of prayer."

People I trained in Amsterdam were practicing sending encouraging voice messages to people they knew. For some reason, they called someone they did not know very well at all. The person responded an hour later and said when they called she was about to attempt suicide. Their message literally saved her life. Now she knew God cared for her and that she was important to Him. Never underestimate the power of an encouraging word because the power of life and death is in our words (see Prov. 18:21)!

Characteristics of God's voice

> For they [God's words] are life to those who find them and health to one's whole body.
> — PROVERBS 4:22 (NIV)

Often people ask me how to test if a prophetic word is from God. One of the best ways is simply to establish how encouraging, strengthening and comforting the word is. During my first year of living in Holland I struggled with discouragement. On more than one occasion I had a friend send me an email detailing a dream they had or simply an encouraging prayer saying God was working everything out for good. Those short notes and emails were life-giving and encouraging for me. They helped me to get through a difficult time.

At a church in Tulsa, Oklahoma, a first-time guest was shocked when I gave him a true message from God. His response was, "God just spoke to me. I have never had that happen before." The next year I was overjoyed to find him and all of his family as faithful members of that church. Hearing God's voice is life-changing.

One American student was coming briefly to Amsterdam. I told her, "God says Europe welcomes you." The next week she arrived in London. But upon arrival she was denied entry to Europe, because she didn't have the right visa! She was taken to a back room. As she waited, she began to take that word

I had given her and said, "Europe welcomes me. I am welcome in Europe." A few minutes later a British immigration officer came in and said, "You don't have the right visa, but we are going to allow you into England. Welcome to Europe."

Encouraging prophetic words help us win life's tough battles. They are like weapons that help us to make it through the difficult times. Like Paul told Timothy, "This charge I entrust to you, Timothy, my child, in accordance with the prophecies previously made about you, that by them you may wage the good warfare" (1 Tim. 1:18).

Another way of discerning God's voice is by listening to the texture or attitude behind the message you are getting. John 10:3-5 says that Jesus goes ahead of us and leads us, calling us by name. He says the sheep do not follow a stranger's voice because they recognize the voice of their shepherd. If a prophetic message is given in an unloving manner full of condemnation, it is probably not from God. John doesn't write that the good shepherd drives and beats his sheep; instead, it says he walks ahead of them and calls them by name. God does not destroy people with His words, He speaks life and light where there is death and darkness.

PROPHESY—*JUST DO IT!*

The best way to learn to swim is by swimming. The best way to learn to play an instrument is by playing an instrument.

From now on, every chapter has exercises to activate and strengthen your ability to prophesy. You can do these exercises individually or with a group. Take a moment to relax and raise up your spiritual antennas. Try one or more of these exercises alone or with a group. Make sure after the exercises you take time to get feedback.

Feedback is vital: you will be able to test your prophetic flow and see where you are accurate and where you may be less accurate. Often we can say things and not have a clue what they mean to the person we are speaking to. So, getting feedback is very important in developing a prophetic ministry which is accountable and transparent.

EXERCISE 1
Prophesy Using Psalm 23 (individual/group)

Open the Bible and read Psalm 23. Read each verse two times and then begin to thank God for what is written in that verse. After praying to God, speak to yourself as if God is speaking to your through the words in the Bible. For example, verse one could lead you to say, "My child, I am your shepherd. I love you and am watching over you. I will take you and guide you wherever I want you to go and I will take care of all your needs. Just as a shepherd cares for his sheep, so I take care of you." Do this with all six verses of Psalm 23.

EXERCISE 2

Journaling God's Answers (individual)

Before you begin, make sure you're sitting comfortably and expect to experience God speaking to you. Start off by simply saying something like, "God, I love You." Then listen to what He says back to you. Ask God questions such as: "God, what do You think of me?', 'God, what do You want to tell me?' Write down what you think God could be telling you. Link what you have written to Bible stories, scriptures or worship songs. Feel free to not only write, but if you want, draw what you experience and place it on paper.

Jesus said if we ask Him for bread, He wouldn't give us a stone (see Matt. 7:9). So, whatever you feel, write it down and then you can test it using Scripture. If it is difficult to get started, write a scripture such as you did in exercise 1 that might be significant to you and then continue to write what God could be saying to you through those words.

EXERCISE 3

Write a Letter to God (individual/group)

A good definition of prayer is telling God what He told us to tell Him. Yes, feel free to read that again! Prayer is a two-way conversation with God. Often, we make the mistake of praying without listening first. Calm yourself down and listen to what God may want to tell you. Write down your prayer to God, beginning with thanksgiving and worshiping Him before you get to your "grocery list" of needs. If you don't know what God wants to tell you, you have a whole

Bible full of words from God to find inspiration; God may well bring to mind a scripture or a Bible story. Write until you cannot write anymore.

EXERCISE 4
Write a Letter from God (individual/group)

Write a letter from God to yourself. Begin the letter with the words, "My dear child," and continue by writing whatever you feel God wants to say to you or someone else. You can sign the letter with the words, "from your heavenly Papa God."

Often God does not speak to us in full sentences but drops words or pictures in our hearts. You may want to write down five to ten heartfelt words and use them to write a letter from God to yourself or to someone else. If you like, you can use these words to write a poem or song.

If you are doing this as a group, have everyone write a letter from God to someone else in the group without knowing for whom it is. Afterwards, shuffle and randomly hand out the letters to different people in the group. See how God speaks to people through this exercise. Do remember that all words from God must be strengthening, encouraging and comforting.

After reading the letters, allow everyone to share what the letters mean to them. As you get more comfortable with this exercise, feel free to do this for friends and even strangers on social media such as Instagram, Facebook or WhatsApp. We are all learning to encourage each other while stepping out of our comfort zones to deliver a message from God to someone else.

EXERCISE 5
Take a Walk with God (individual)
In Genesis 3:8, God is walking through the garden of Eden, longing to talk to Adam and Eve. A great way to experience God's presence is by taking a walk with Him in nature (Ps. 19:1). Do not be rushed but enjoy meandering through a forest or strolling on a beach. Talk to God and listen to what He may say to you through what you see.

EXERCISE 6
Sing a Prophecy (individual/group)
Sing a song to God and then sing a song as if it is God singing over you or others present in the room. This can lead to new songs being written. Often, great authority is released with prophetic music.

King David was a prophetic psalmist. Worship leaders with a strong prophetic gifting should release songs prophetically. In his ministry, my brother has seen powerful manifestations of God's presence when someone begins prophesying through song. Demons begin manifesting, people are set free. Prophetic worship is powerful!

EXERCISE 7
Do a Prophetic Act or Motion (group)
Have a person stand up and use a motion to prophesy. Possible motions include: having them turn around, placing a crown on their head, lifting their hands, stomping on the ground, clapping their hands, washing feet or kneeling. One of the most powerful prophetic acts is simply appropriately hugging someone so they can experience the embrace of their heavenly Father.

The Bible is full of prophetic acts that prophets did to illustrate what God was going to do. Ezekiel dug a hole through the city wall (see Ezek. 12:5). Hosea married Gomer, an unfaithful prostitute, whom he kept getting to come home (see Hos. 1:2-3). Jesus washed the feet of His disciples, and He blew on them to receive the Holy Spirit (see John 13:1-7; 20:22). Taking Holy Communion is one of the most powerful prophetic acts there is. There is great power in prophetic acts.

CHAPTER 2

Keys

Now I want you all to speak in tongues, but even more to prophesy.
— 1 CORINTHIANS 14:5a

The LORD your God is in your midst, a mighty one who will save; he will rejoice over you with gladness; he will quiet you by his love; he will exult over you with loud singing.
— ZEPHANIAH 3:17

Prophecy is more than hearing God's voice, it is speaking his words. It means you tell someone what you think He wants to say to that person.

When my daughter, Hannah, was born, her mother had lost too much blood to be able to hold her in her arms. My sweet little girl came out crying at the top of her lungs, as all new-born babies should. When the nurses handed her to me, I started singing the song my father sang over me: "I love Hannah. I love Hannah, yes, I do. Yes, I do. She is very special. She is very special. Yes, she is. Yes, she is."

The moment she heard my voice, she stopped crying because she recognized the voice of her father singing over her. I had sung and spoken over her when she was inside of her mother's belly.

When our youngest, Benjamin, was a baby, there were times when he would stop crying when his big sister Hannah would sing over him: "I love Benjamin. I love Benjamin. Yes, I do. Yes, I do. He is very special. He is very special. Yes, he is." This is a wonderful picture of what God wants us to share with people. When we prophesy, we speak God's words. We are singing the song of love over others; the one God continually sings over us.

My message is the same everywhere. Every week when we go to the windows of Amsterdam's Red-light District, we tell the women: "God loves you and He has good plans of hope and a future for you. You are valuable. God wants you to have the experience of being His beloved child. God wants to sing His love over you." This is a universal message. God desires that everyone come to know Him as their true source of life. Prophecy is meant to be a blessing to everyone, a reflection of God's loving heart.

In Numbers 11:24-30 we read a story of seventy elders of Israel who began prophesying when the Holy Spirit came upon them. All of them prophesied at the assigned tent where they were to meet Moses, except for Eldad and Medad. They remained in their homes. To Joshua's horror, these two elders were prophesying freely at the wrong location. He demanded Moses silence them immediately. Moses unexpectedly responded to Joshua by saying, "Are you jealous for my sake? Would that all the LORD's people were prophets, that the LORD would put his Spirit on them!" (Num. 11:29).

This amazing narrative is a preview of the day of Pentecost, when God would pour out His Spirit upon all flesh. But there is more to the story: it also has an important key hidden in the names of Eldad and Medad. Eldad's name means "God has loved" and Medad's name means "love."[4] In other words: whenever and wherever we prophesy, we must prophesy in love. To Prophecy without love is meaningless.

Paul makes this clear in 1 Corinthians 13 when he says: "If I speak in the tongues of men and of angels, but have not love, I am a noisy gong or a clanging cymbal. And if I have prophetic powers, and understand all mysteries and all knowledge, and if I have all faith, so as to remove mountains, but have not love, I am nothing. If I give away all I have, and if I deliver up my body to be burned, but have not love, I gain nothing" (1 Cor. 13:1-3).

In January 2016, one of my best friends learned that prophecy is all about God's love. I took a Dutch ministry team to do a prophetic youth conference in Budapest, Hungary. My friend came along. He comes from a traditional Christian background where he had heard very little about prophesying. When I told him he was going to prophesy, he told me he was going to watch me and learn but by no means was he ready to prophesy.

At the end of the first meeting, fifty people lined up to receive prophetic ministry. I stood there with an interpreter. My friend was on the other side watching and listening as I prophesied over the first individual. Then I simply walked away and left him there with a line waiting to receive a word from God!

He started prophesying over all of those people and afterward told me, "Matt, this was so easy. All I had to do was love these people the way God loves me. It was so easy and so amazing!" I knew he was already full of love, Scripture, and the Spirit of God. For him, prophesying would be very natural and easy.

So how can we align ourselves with God's love, and share it with the people around us? What are the key factors for sound prophesying?

Desire God's Presence More Than His Presents

Some years ago, I was wide awake in bed at 2 a.m. I was in Chicago for a month, suffering from jet lag and really missing my wife and my children. Suddenly the following thought came to me: "I do miss my family, and I want to be with them, but I am going to focus my thoughts on God. Yes, God, I want You. I really want to see and experience You now. I long for You." That month changed my life. I experienced God profoundly as I set my desire on Him. I learned that the key to growing in prophecy is seeking God's presence more than His presents.

One time I drove down I-44 expressway to Oklahoma City. I cranked up worship music and suddenly felt God was there. Jesus was in the car with me, and I could feel Him. His presence is amazing! During that month in Chicago, I organized two days of prayer and fasting where I taught and prophesied over people for hours. Yet prophesying was not what was most significant; it was experiencing God's presence.

Later that year, in Madill, Oklahoma, I organized another day of prayer and fasting and once again the manifest presence of God showed up. A divine silence covered the church sanctuary. We knew God was in the room in a tangible way. Nobody needed to say anything, because God was there.

We do not *need* to feel God's presence because we walk by faith and not by what we feel (2 Cor. 5:7). However, we *can* feel and experience God, and it is a great blessing. That's why I once offered some tourists looking for drugs in Amsterdam some "really good stuff." I told them what I had was the best stuff possible. When I explained it was knowing Jesus, they scoffed at me, but they did tell me I was a good salesman. What they did not realize was my offer was completely true. There is no high like knowing Jesus!

I have also experienced God's presence and have learned to discern His presence in less spectacular, more mundane moments. I can see Him in nature, my children and many other places which may seem unimportant or unspiritual. All in all, I understand David's words when he says,

> One thing have I asked of the LORD, that I will seek after: that I may dwell in the house of the LORD all the days of my life, to gaze upon the beauty of the LORD.
> – PSALMS 27:4

If we go after God because we want *stuff* from Him, we could be in trouble. Simon the sorcerer offered Peter money to have the ability to lay hands on people so they could be filled with the Holy Spirit. Peter rebuked him harshly (see Acts 8:20-25). We do not go after gifts from God first, we go after Him. As God fills our lives with His presence, the presents of His Spirit (like healing, prophecy and tongues) become normal and natural. But His presence is the greatest present we can ever have.

Keep Your House from Leaning

Downtown Amsterdam is filled with picturesque historical buildings, many of which were built in the seventeenth or eighteenth century. Though beautiful, many of them are crooked and leaning. The soft ground in Amsterdam makes buildings shift if they are not built on poles which go deep into the ground. Without that foundation, the buildings will fall, leading to possible death and destruction. Likewise, ministry gifting or anointing needs the foundation of integrity and Christ-like character development. Without it, it will start to lean, leading to destruction.

Some individuals who have had powerful ministries have appeared and disappeared like shooting stars. It is good to develop a strong anointing or gifting but learn to keep your eyes focused on heaven with your feet solidly planted on the ground. Your character should be able to carry your ministry. Be honest, pay your bills, be responsible, and treat your friends and family members with kindness.

If you want to grow in supernatural ministry, you cannot isolate yourself. Have friends who will speak the *truth* to you, no matter how much God uses you. Have people in your life with whom you can be transparent and who can help you when you need it. Many people who have a strong prophetic gifting can struggle with depression and discouragement. I have never felt alone because I have intentionally nurtured mutually accountable relationships with great friends. They care for me because of who I am and not what I can do. It is vital to create accountability structures and cultivate relationships with people who can pray, listen and advise you.

Also, be very careful who you get romantically involved with. Church history is full of examples of Christians who get romantically involved with someone who ultimately puts out their desire to serve God and use their spiritual gifts. It is better to be alone than to be married to the wrong person. Taking this advice can save you a lot of heartache.

You become like the people who are closest to you so be sure to find people who can make you stronger and better. My greatest success in life was marrying Femke. She is a woman who is constantly through her love, faith and devotion, making me a better husband, father, minister and individual.

Another key character trait to strive for is humility. Moses and Jesus are the best models of effective prophetic ministry and they were both humble. Jesus said, "learn from me, for I am gentle and lowly in heart, and you will find rest for your souls" (see Matt. 11:29). We reflect Jesus, and He is "gentle and

lowly in heart." When we look at Jesus, we see our heavenly
Father (see John 14:9). Jesus is God the Father's selfie! As followers
of Jesus, we must be able to say to others, "Be imitators of me,
as I am of Christ" (1 Cor. 11:1). When I am prideful, rude or
arrogant, I am not reflecting Him.

Often when I come into a new church, I literally follow
the example Jesus gave us: I will wash the feet of the leader
present. To model the true prophetic ministry is to serve the
leaders of the local church. We are there to serve the body and
not to lord our will over others. The greatest prophets in the
Bible were humble, and that is our standard.

Jonathan Edwards once gave a wonderful description of
what pride and humility look like. He placed the two as polar
opposites against each other. The chart here illustrates what
pride and humility is.[5]

Pride is...	Humility is...
being driven by emptiness or fear.	being content.
being disrespectful to people who think or act differently than yourself.	being kind, friendly and respectful even to people who are different than yourself.
being unteachable, a know-it-all.	being teachable and correctable.
being insecure.	being secure.
destructive.	life-giving.

Pray in Tongues Often

Praying or speaking in tongues (also called praying in the Spirit) is a fantastic way to prepare for prophetic and healing ministry. It is a way of stirring up the gift of God inside of you (see 2 Tim. 1:6). I know many prophets and healing evangelists who regularly spend many hours praying in tongues (see 1 Cor. 14:15). It can help you to get the prophetic flow going.

Let me briefly explain this. Paul said he wanted everyone to pray in tongues, but he desired more that they would prophesy (1 Cor. 14:5). Praying in tongues or in the Spirit means praying to God in an unknown human language (1 Cor. 14:2). It is a way of building yourself up (Jude 1:20). It is also a vital part of the armor of God (Eph. 6:18). Although there may be moments where a person can literally begin speaking another human language unknown to him or herself (see Acts 2:1-12), most of the time a person is uttering sounds and syllables which make no sense to the human mind. Paul describes this as praying mysteries by the Spirit (1 Cor. 14:2).

We do not pray in tongues or prophesy from our own thinking, but from our spirit. Our spirit knows our thoughts and the Holy Spirit knows God's thoughts. When the Holy Spirit lives in us, then we can receive the thoughts and mind of Christ (1 Cor. 2:6-16). For the secular mind this seems all foolishness (1 Cor. 2:14). We can connect to God's Spirit that lives in us when we allow Him to speak through us, through a tongue or a prophetic message. It is like a river of living water flowing from our inside to others (John 7:37-39).

I was raised praying in tongues in my family. Whenever my father would travel to another country to do healing services, he would spend a day fasting and praying in a hotel. He would pray in tongues all day long. This built him up, but also helped him to minister for the following days. Praying in tongues is a powerful tool for ministry.

If you want to begin speaking in tongues, ask God for this gift. He will not give you a stone, scorpion or snake if you ask him for a piece of bread, an egg or fish (Luke 11:9-13). He is a good and generous father. Like prophesying, the hardest part of speaking in tongues is getting started. Ask God to fill you and cleanse you with his Holy Spirit. Then by faith, begin to speak in a new tongue. For some, this may be only one or two new syllables. Just as a baby who is learning a new language, you may only repeat two or more words. The more you do it though, the more it grows.[6]

Some people I know have started speaking in tongues at their home while sitting on their couch or laying in their bed. Carol Wimber tells a very unique and funny story of how she began speaking in tongues. In a dream she was giving a seven-point message on why speaking in tongues is not for today. She woke up speaking in tongues. God went past her understanding through her spirit and she began praying in the Spirit.[7]

Every believer who wants this gift to be activated in their lives can receive it. For many, it is helpful to have someone else pray for them, lay hands on them and bless them. Do not be afraid or uptight but relax. Open your mouth and God will fill it (Ps. 81:10).

Praying in the Spirit is not necessary for salvation or acceptance from God. It does not make a person a superior believer. It is simply another gift from God to empower us to do His work and be His witnesses (Acts 1:8). Like the Ephesian believers, many believers are unaware that these gifts are available for everyone who asks. Speaking in tongues and prophecy are a normal result of being filled with the Holy Spirit (Acts 19:1-7).

I have seen people who begin speaking in tongues or start prophesying, but then stop because of fear. They are afraid it is just themselves making up sounds and saying things. But you can continue praying in the Spirit and trusting God that these sounds are not just you. Trust that the Holy Spirit is praying through you in accordance with the will of God (Rom. 8:26-27).

One woman told me, "So you are saying I should open up my mouth and talk gibberish. I should just by faith talk like a baby." Though that may be a little oversimplified, my answer was yes. We open our mouths and trust that the gibberish we speak is the Spirit giving us a new prayer language.

God will never force us to prophesy or speak in a new tongue. I am the one who decides when I will open my mouth and pray in tongues or give a prophetic word. If you wait for God to come and force you to speak in tongues or prophesy, you probably won't do either. Ask God and by faith receive and release this spiritual gift.

When you pray in tongues, also ask God to interpret what you are praying (1 Cor. 14:15). Often when I am praying in tongues, I will change into a known language and amazing things may come out of my mouth.

Relax and Don't Be Weird

Make a tight fist with your right hand and see how difficult it is to stick a finger from your left hand into that fist. Now relax and open your right hand wide and see how easy it is to move your left fingers into your right hand. If you want to hear God's voice clearly, *relax* and be at *rest*. Being at rest makes it easier for God to speak to us and lead us when we prophesy. Trusting God and being relaxed when prophesying is beneficial for everyone who gives and hears a prophetic word.

A word from God does not need to be delivered with an emotional charge or with King James English. Once you begin flowing prophetically, God's thoughts will sound just like your own thoughts. The only way to find out if they are from Him is to say what you are seeing, thinking, or feeling, and then ask if what we are saying makes any sense.

I am concerned about people I know who have shied away from prophecy and spiritual gifts because they saw some people being flaky and weird. If God is my Father, then it is normal that He will speak to me. I do not speak to my children in King James English or get spooky with them (unless I am playing with them). So, we can talk to people conversationally and share what we feel God is saying.

One day I walked into my son's pre-school class and saw a picture for the teacher. I wrote an encouraging note and described what I saw. The next day, I saw the note taped onto the wall. I did not write, "So says the Lord..." I just encouraged her with the words I felt God wanted to speak to her. She appreciated it so much she put it up so everyone could see what I had written. Prophetic ministry is not only for a church context, but for daily "normal" life. It can easily be done in an everyday way.

Flow Like a Kleenex Box

You may get one picture, word, scripture, impression, or maybe absolutely nothing when you pray for a person. But as you begin to pray by faith, words may begin to flow out of your mouth like a stream of living water. When you say that one scripture or picture, more may come. The dam may break and a prophetic flow may begin to develop.

Like a tissue in a Kleenex box, when you pull one out, more comes. When you start speaking words of life, more can come. Many times when I begin to prophesy, I do not know what I am going to say. But I trust God that when I open my mouth, He will fill it (see Ps. 81:10).

One day my wife was prophesying over a daughter and a mother. Femke suddenly heard songs and saw pictures from the daughter's childhood. As she began telling them about what she saw and heard, the two began to weep. These were cherished memories that due to traumatic events had been forgotten. Now the memories began to come back.

Fear will hinder us from prophesying. We want to be in control and know everything we are going to say ahead of time so as to not make a mistake. Nearly every time I train groups in prophetic ministry, someone freezes up and says something like: "I can't do this. This is too difficult" or, "I want it to be God and not me."

When it comes to faith, God does not necessarily give that kind of certainty. Prophesying often means speaking words and not knowing what I am going to say. It is like the step the priests had to make when the people of Israel crossed the river Jordan after wandering in the desert for forty years. When crossing the Jordan, the priests had to step into a deep and dangerous flooding river. It was only as their feet touched the water that the river began to recede (Josh. 3:13-16). God will speak through your lips when you open your mouth and not before.

Two Hebrew words for prophesying have to do with flowing like water. The first is *nataph*, which means to ooze, to distill gradually, to fall in drops, or to speak in inspiration. This is a beautiful picture of how during worship or prayer, thoughts and pictures can fall like rain into our spirits.

The second word for prophecy is *naba*. It has a sense of "bubbling or springing up, flowing, pouring out or gushing forth".[8] It is like a river of inspiration that flows from our spirits as we prophesy (see John 4:14; 7:38-39). Often, when I first begin training people in prophetic ministry, they are reticent and insecure. As they grow, however, a strong steady prophetic flow can develop.

I prophesy quickly. But there are many styles of prophets and many ways to prophesy. The task you have is to connect to God and discern how God speaks to you and through you. This is best developed together with experienced prophets and other people learning how to prophesy.

Sometimes when I am prophesying I feel very vulnerable. I feel like I am standing in my underwear. I don't know people, and I don't know what I should tell them. Fortunately, I don't have to know what to say because I prophesy from my spirit and not from my intellect. Once I get over the initial hurdles of fear and start prophesying, I may step into a prophetic river where words, pictures, and thoughts begin to flow rapidly. At that point, my mind is filled with God's thoughts, which feels so natural that it's just as if they were my own thoughts.

The challenge remains filtering those thoughts in an appropriate manner: I must communicate those words in a way that strengthens, encourages, and comforts someone. I should also articulate the message in a way they can understand. This is where developing the skill of prophesying comes into it. Just as someone can grow in their teaching ability, so they can grow in their ability to prophesy. Part of this involves using "Prophetic Hermeneutics."

Use Prophetic Hermeneutics

Hermeneutics is the term theologians use to explain the process of interpreting the Bible. The three steps used to understanding Scripture are also the same steps used for "unpacking" prophecy: Revelation, Interpretation and Application. All three are essential: a correct revelation with the wrong interpretation or wrong application will lead to wrong results. A correct revelation and a correct interpretation with the wrong application will lead to frustration.

Once I sat in a car with a friend of mine who told me about his daughter wanting to go to another country, yet she was having trouble getting a visa. When I saw her a few minutes later, I saw a green light and an eagle soaring high. I didn't ask the Lord for an explanation, but immediately gave her my own interpretation. I told her she was going to get the visa and travel to that nation, but I was wrong. Shortly afterward, she was denied the visa and was extremely disappointed. I had to apologize to her and fortunately she forgave me. This also illustrates why I prefer not knowing anything about a person before I prophesy over them so I will not confuse what I know with what I feel God is speaking about them at that moment.

A *revelation* can be a picture or a scripture, the meaning of which you may have no idea. But as you begin to unpack the revelation (like scripture, a picture or a dream), the Holy Spirit can give you the interpretation and possibly also the application.

Years ago, while prophesying over a woman, God began highlighting her hair to me. I had no clue what it meant, but as I began speaking about her, I said, "You are a worshiper just like the woman who dried the feet of Jesus with her hair. You are a person who truly worships the Lord in Spirit and in truth." This word proved to be true about her. After revelation came interpretation.

Just as there are many helpful resources in being able to interpret Scripture, so there are some great resources on dream and vision interpretation. Nevertheless, the best way to learn to interpret a revelation is through prayer. Ask God what He wants to say through a word, picture, or dream. Write it down and perhaps the interpretation will become clear later. Do not be in a hurry to figure out what everything means at that moment.

Recently at an evening for practicing prophecy, someone walked up to me with a star from a Christmas tree, saying, "I believe that you are like a star which people from the East are going to seek to find Jesus." What he did not know was that I had just been asked by leaders from Eastern Europe to come and train them in Power Evangelism. He gave me the revelation, and I was able to interpret it immediately and apply it to my life.

Sometimes you may get a revelation but not know how a person needs to interpret it or apply it. Once, I saw a woman as a mother hen with a lot of little chicks around her. I told her this and then asked her what it meant to her. She responded, "I work at a daycare center, and I have been asking God if I should keep working with these children. Your picture was an answer to my prayer." Finally, application.

Once I was in Hungary, and I told a young woman she was going to do prophetic ministry with me. I thought this meant she would join my prophetic ministry team. She did indeed become a part of my prophetic ministry team, but it was different than I thought: she was the person who organized the first youth prophetic conference in Hungary.

Years ago, I told a young Romanian woman she was going to work in the fashion industry and that she would be a top manager for an international company. She did not feel as if my words applied to her at all with her ambitions and desires. That was until years later while working at the Italian multinational fashion company in Germany as a manager, she remembered the prophetic word. Though she did not understand it at the time of receiving it, it truly came to pass.

I prophesied over a young couple that they were going to travel throughout all of Europe doing evangelism. At the time they thought that was a word for when they were old and retired. Three years later, they built a home on wheels and have traveled throughout Europe preaching the gospel. It was then that they recalled the word I had given them years earlier.

In 2010, someone prophesied that God was going to use me as a leader in the United States. I immediately rejected that word because I lived in the Netherlands and didn't plan on living in the United States. That year, I spent four months in the USA and God used me as a leader there. Now in 2018, I am seeing how God is using me as a leader in the USA while living in Amsterdam.

Misuse of a revelation is possible. I was at a church once when I prophesied over a man that he was a leader and God was going to use him as a king to lead many people. That man took the prophetic word and tried to split the church using the word I gave him. The pastor, who is a good friend of mine, told me, "Matt, everything that you said about him was true, but he used that word in a wrong way and at the wrong time."

We need to respond to revelation according to God's timing. That's what David did. There was a gap of about twenty years between when Samuel anointed David to become the king of Israel and when David was actually crowned king. David did not go out immediately to kill Saul and become king in his own strength and time. David is an excellent example of someone who knew and respected God's timing.

Jesus also showed He followed God's timing: He began His ministry at the age of thirty, and it only lasted three years. All of the Messianic prophecies of the Old Testament were waiting to be fulfilled, and He fulfilled all of them in the proper window of time.

God is more interested in who we are than what we will do for Him. A prophetic word can be for now, a year from now, or decades from now. This is why we must not be too quick to disqualify a prophetic word we do not understand. If you don't know what to do with it, you can *always* allow God to make you into the person through whom He will bring that word to pass.

Deliver the Prophetic Pizza

When you prophesy, you are a spokesperson for God. Your job is similar to a pizza delivery person—you deliver what God is saying and don't make people comply or accept it. You would be unhappy if a delivery person forced you to eat the pizza when they wanted you to. Give people space to judge the word and decide for themselves what they are or are not going to do with the message. People are responsible for their own lives and they must be able to choose what they will do or not do after receiving a prophetic word.

Another thing: no one wants to eat a pizza delivered in a cold cardboard box full of holes and dirt. The box would take away from the edibility of the pizza. In the same way, don't let your presentation get in the way of what God wants to say to a person. Present a message from God in a way that will not take away from the message itself. Be aware of appropriate dress when serving people of other cultures. Don't express your political opinions when prophesying. Use language and expressions people will understand. Avoid secondary or non-important details which can distract from a message which comes from God. Our job is to do our best to present a message from God people can understand and digest.

Get Feedback

As a delivery person, be open to getting feedback on how your "prophetic pizza" is understood or experienced. Don't be too excited when everything you say is 100 percent accurate, and don't be too discouraged when it's not. We are all learning in this, and maintaining open communication with God and those we serve is crucial for growing in the prophetic.

The influential American Bible teacher Kenneth Hagin was praying for a young man and suddenly he heard the words coming out of his mouth: "This is a confirmation of what I said to you at three o'clock this afternoon as you were praying in the storm cellar. You asked for a confirmation, and this is it. That was Me speaking to you." After the service he asked him, "Were you praying down in the storm cellar at three o'clock this afternoon?" He was. At that moment, he was asking God for a confirmation of whether he should become a preacher. He felt God told him at that moment, "I will give you a confirmation tonight." Hagin's words were his confirmation.[9]

Often, I ask people, "Does that make sense?" This way I can learn myself, but also I do not always know the meaning of what I am saying. Do not be concerned with how profound or impressive you appear. Some of the simplest words can have a significant meaning you may be unaware of.

One day I got the word "cookie" for a woman. I asked her, "What does that mean?" She said her grandfather's nickname was Cookie and he was a great man of faith. She loved him dearly, and her prayer was that his faith would continue in her children. It was very significant to her that I began un- knowingly talking about her grandfather while talking about her faith.

Whenever I minister prophetically, I try to use an evaluation form where people can give me feedback about prophetic ministry they have received from me or one of my teams. In Holland, I commonly get a 60-100 percent accuracy rate on the prophetic words I give to people. I would love to say I am always 100 percent accurate in everything I say. But it is great in always keeping me humble, especially if someone gives me a 10 percent rating on accuracy. It forces me to be sensitive to what God is saying now and not just base what I have done or said in the past.

Do Not Get Stuck in a Rut

Realize how God uses you today may not be how He chooses to use you tomorrow. In Exodus 17:6, God tells Moses to strike a rock and water comes out of it. However, in Numbers 20:8-12, he tells Moses to speak to a rock. Moses disobeys and hits it like he had previously. Strategies and ministry methods are good, but they do not replace our personal responsibility to listen and obey God.

At times on the street I have gotten a bunch of accurate words of knowledge for strangers. I have started to feel confident and then the next person would say I was totally wrong. Do not trust your previous experience, your successes or failures, but listen and trust God. Do what you feel He tells you to do.

In Numbers 21:4-9, God tells Moses to use a bronze snake on a stick to heal people who have been bitten by poisonous snakes. Then in 2 Kings 18:4 we read that the Israelites were actually worshiping that bronze snake instead of God. Most people who experience a move of God proceed to reject new moves of God among other people because it does not look or feel like what they have experienced with God. Do not get stuck in a rut and place God in a box. This book may be describing things which are outside of your ministry experience. Do not reject it because it is unfamiliar to you. God is extremely creative and He can use other forms of music, art and ministry than what you are used to.

Practice Makes Perfect

The first time I played the guitar, it sounded horrible. Now, because of lots of hours of practice, I can lead a church in praise and worship. When you first start prophesying, it may not sound very confident, perfect, or smooth. Don't let that impede you. Keep learning, studying, watching, growing and developing in prophetic ministry. Remain loving, humble and teachable and see how you can grow in prophecy. Learn to hear God's voice and speak His words. Prophesy!

When Stuck, Use a Diving Board

God's thoughts about us outnumber all of the grains of sand on the seashore (see Ps. 139:18). He is generous and creative in speaking to us. However, there may be times when you have no clue what to say. You are totally blank. The hardest part of prophesying at times is getting started. Grab any random object and use it as a "diving board." Sometimes I will ask a woman to give me a random object out of her purse or use a phone number, license plate, or dream to prophesy. The most important thing is not the object I use, but the ability God has to speak to us through anything.

Two people with strong prophetic gifting accompanied me to Budapest for a conference. During a three-hour break, we walked around town and practiced prophesying over each other using the signs and things we saw during our walk. This loosened them up, and their prophetic flow became much stronger after that exercise. Prophesying takes simple, child-like faith. Using a diving board can help you if or when you get stuck.

Prophesy Together

I do not like to do ministry by myself. I always like to take others with me. This is mutually beneficial, as the spiritual anointing can be contagious. I like to invest in other people's lives because it is most beneficial for myself. The best way to grow in prophecy is by prophesying and teaching others how to prophesy.

When John Wimber realized signs and wonders were following his ministry everywhere he went, he found himself facing a decision. He once told his wife, Carol, "I can either get a tent and have a huge revival where I can do this by myself, or I can release it to the people, and equip them to play."[10] He chose the latter, and because of that had a much larger impact than he would have had he did everything himself.

Prophecy and the gifts of the Holy Spirit are not just for "special anointed" people. They are for every believer. Whenever I travel, I always try to take a team of people who do the ministry with me, modeling the strategy of Jesus and the apostle Paul. Don't hold onto ministry for yourself, but release ministry into the hands of other believers. We don't lose but *gain* authority by giving it away to others.

Like I said, the best way to grow in spiritual gifts is by training others how they can use them. I celebrate and rejoice when those who I have mentored see amazing healings and miracles I have not seen yet. It is not about me, it is all about Jesus. And like Jesus I regularly say, "Everything I can do, you can do better."

It's great if you can find a mentor to help you grow in prophecy. But if you are in a church or a place where you don't have any mentors, do not worry. I have never met most of my mentors! I have never met John Wimber, Oral Roberts, Timothy Keller, Ignatius of Loyola, T.L. Osborn, the apostle Peter, or apostle Paul. I have read their writings, though, and they have helped shaped my life and ministry today. Read good books and then find people with whom you can do more than just talk about what you read but *do* what they *did*.

Desire to grow in spiritual gifts by not just talking about them, but by stepping out and using them. When I first came to Amsterdam, we set up monthly men's prayer meetings where we would simply pray for each other. Often, as we prayed, God would speak through us. Some of those men are now my best friends and ministry partners. They have given me many valuable words from God on many occasions.

Bring Out the Best in Others

I was biking with my daughter after watching a Charlie Brown film. She surprised me by saying, "Papa, the little red-haired girl is a prophet just like you. Right, Papa?"

Everyone in *The Peanuts Movie* has the tendency to treat poor Charlie Brown badly. Lucy is constantly pulling away the football when he wants to kick it, people make fun of him, and he feels like a big loser. But at the end of the movie, to his own amazement, the little red-haired girl wants to be his pen pal. She wants to be his pen pal because he is honest, funny, smart, sincere and caring. She strengthens, encourages and comforts him, leaving Charlie Brown and the viewer with a warm feeling. My daughter equated this heart-warming experience to all of the meetings she has had with prophets. Prophets speak God's truth in love and bring out the best in other people. A prophet's greatest goal is not to prophesy, but to love people the same way that God loves us. Focus on Jesus and loving people and prophesying becomes easy and natural.

PROPHESY—*JUST DO IT!*

EXERCISE 1
Pray in the Spirit (individual/group)

Thank God that Jesus is the Lord of your life and that you are His child (John 1:12). Thank Him for His Spirit and the gifts He has available to you. Ask Him to cleanse you and forgive you of all sin. Then ask Him to fill you with His Holy Spirit and help you activate the gift of speaking in tongues. Relax and then by faith begin speaking in a new language you do not know. Once you begin praying in tongues expect to see more of His gifts develop in your life. Take your time to pray in tongues, but also in a language you do know.

EXERCISE 2
Interpret a Tongue (individual/group)

Once you pray in tongues, ask God to give you the interpretation to what you are praying. Pray in the Spirit and then pray in a language you understand. Do this for yourself or for others when they pray in tongues.

EXERCISE 3
Get the Picture (individual/group)

By faith, ask God for a picture. This is as simple as a picture we see with our mind's eye (the eye of our imagination). When you see a picture, describe it and then by faith begin to share what you believe God could be saying through that picture. Follow the prophetic guidelines as you deliver this word. A picture is worth a thousand words and that is why God loves to speak through pictures. The dreams, pictures and visions He has given remain with me for a long time. You never know when a picture is symbolic or a word of knowledge. While prophesying over a group of students, I told a woman she was like a nurse and I saw her taking care of babies. I then found out she was studying to be a midwife. Tell what you see and say what you think it means. Then find out what it means to your listener.

EXERCISE 4
Prophesy Scripture (group)

Begin with a scripture passage such as Psalm 139 and have team members read that passage and use it to begin prophesying over the person next to them. Random Scripture cards can also be used to help people get started. The goal, however, is for participants to be able to prophesy using Scripture that is in their own heart – they do not need to know where a scripture is found. Just quote it and speak it forth as if it is God speaking those very words to their hearers.

The Bible is the inspired Word of God, and we can have a higher level of confidence when interpreting and applying Scripture to people's lives. I am amazed how often God speaks through Scripture. One Sunday I visited a church. After the service I walked up to a man and said, "The just shall live by faith" (Heb. 10:38 NKJV). He later told me how for an entire week the Lord had been speaking to him through that scripture.

EXERCISE 5
Go to God's Throne Using Revelation 4 (individual)

Hebrews 4:16 says we can approach God's throne to find mercy and grace whenever we may need it. Thankfully we have a full detailed description of God's throne in Revelation 4. Read this chapter three to four times and then begin to imagine everything you read. Imagine yourself as one of the twenty-four elders casting your crown before God's throne. You may even want to prostrate yourself on the ground and worship God as if you are doing what they are doing. Take the words of the elders or the four living creatures around His throne and use them to worship God yourself. Learn how you can come before God's throne at any time and any place whenever you need help. Use this passage to pray to our God who is seated on the throne.

EXERCISE 6

Random Object (group)

Have people in the group pick out a random object and use it to deliver a prophetic word to someone in the room. The leader of the group can also call out a random object whereby participants may prophesy. This exercise is excellent in helping people relax and know what to do when they feel they are stuck. If they are stuck, they can by faith grab a random object which serves as a diving board to start prophesying.

Once, one individual used a cup of water to give twelve different people an accurate word. The secret is not in the object that you use, but in your ability to hear God's voice no matter what the object may be.

A friend of mine did not understand this activation, so I told him to name a random object in the room. He said, "The dog's bed." I then started prophesying that God was calling him to rest in His presence as a dog rests in its bed. He then responded that the previous night three people had prayed for him and all said God wanted him to rest.

EXERCISE 7

Walk Through a City and Prophesy Over Each Other (group)

Walk through a city with one or more people and prophesy over each other using whatever you may see on your walk. Use the signs, colors and landmarks to strengthen, encourage and comfort one another. This is an excellent exercise to get people's prophetic flow going so they are not afraid to open their mouths and prophesy.

CHAPTER 3

Barriers

One of the greatest barriers Christians have to prophesying is that they do not understand prophecy. If I was to define "prophecy" simply as listening prayer, generally there would be less resistance to using the word. In effect, listening prayer is a wonderful description of prophetic ministry, yet there is so much more to simply listening to God as we pray. Prophetic ministry is for every believer. In this chapter I focus on getting rid of the barriers which impede individuals from being comfortable with prophecy.

An Unbiblical World View

One reason many believers do not experience a dynamic relationship with God is their world view is based more upon ideas from the eighteenth century Enlightenment than from Scripture. Four big ideas from that time are atheism, deism, rationalism, materialism and individualism.[11]

Atheism is the idea God does not exist. Deism says *if* He exists, He is not involved in our daily lives. Instead, He is more of a Creator who, like a clockmaker, set things in motion but is otherwise uninvolved in His creation. Rationalism says if you cannot rationally explain something, you should not trust it. Rationalism rules out all biblical and modern miracles (the virgin birth, the resurrected Savior and divine healing). People who subscribe to a purely rationalistic viewpoint presuppose that we live in a closed world system in which the supernatural does not and cannot exist.

Materialism says only what you can experience with your five senses exists. Many funerals I have attended in the Netherlands never mention anything about life after death, since materialism implies once a person dies, it's all over. Individualism is the idea it is most important you believe in yourself first above any other person or ideas. This individualism, taken to the extreme, engenders not only pride but greed, selfishness and all the kinds of brokenness our world experiences today. Western cultures are far greater adherents to the Enlightenment than to the teachings of the Bible. And many Christians have unknowingly bought into these ideas. Their core beliefs are not from the Bible, but their culture.

The Bible reveals a personal God who desires to interact with us daily and is intimately familiar with every detail of our lives, including the very number of hairs on our heads (see Luke 12:7). He teaches using our five senses is important, yet there is much more than what our five physical senses can experience or understand (see Eph. 3:20). We are body, soul and spirit. Through our spirits we can personally know God and learn to use our spiritual senses as well as our physical ones.

The Bible also explains that though it may be important to have a healthy self-image, the purpose of our existence is to live in community with God and with others. "No man is an island"—as John Donne's poem tells us—and everyone longs for a perfect and unconditional love which can only be found through knowing Jesus Christ. Knowing Jesus awakens the supernatural element in our lives which makes living for God both natural and supernatural.

Old Testament-based Prophecy

Another barrier is people confuse Old Testament prophecy with New Testament prophecy. In the Old Testament, prophets generally declared judgment, and if they made a mistake, they could be put to death (see Deut. 18:20-22). In the New Testament, prophecy is primarily believers strengthening, encouraging, and comforting one another. There is no death penalty hanging on the necks of those who don't prophesy accurately. However, every prophetic word *must* be evaluated and tested to determine what is from God and what is not (see 1 Cor. 14:29; 1 Thess. 5:19-22).

Not understanding the difference between Old Testament and New Testament prophecy is a common barrier preventing people from growing in prophetic ministry. Who is going to prophesy if you are afraid of making a mistake and being put to death as a false prophet? How can a person develop in this ministry if they have no sound paradigm for New Testament prophecy? This book is an attempt at laying down a sound and biblical structure for developing prophetic ministry.

When people prophesy, preach, or do evangelism using an Old Testament paradigm, they can be highly destructive. Understanding grace and the gospel of Jesus Christ is extremely important for those who speak God's words. The gospel is not about changing your outward behavior or appearance but your heart being transformed by the love and grace of God. Prophecy should never destroy people or a church. It should serve to build the Church up (see 1 Cor. 14:4).

All the gifts of the Spirit are about love, and when we fail in this, we have missed the whole point. In his book *School of the Prophets*, Kris Vallotton tells a story which illustrates this.[12] One Sunday in 1998, the new pastor at his home church asked the people to go to those they needed to forgive for things they had said or done in the past. To Vallotton's horror, a long line of people came up to him to tell him about incidents when he had given them an accurate prophetic word which had ended up causing them problems because he delivered them in an unloving fashion. He realized that day that giving an accurate word in an unloving and ungracious spirit can be devastating. It does not accomplish God's will.

I experienced something like this myself. I felt insulted by a leader and rebuked him for his "lack of faith and vision." Later that year, I had to call him back and apologize for disrespecting him and his ministry in that way. He graciously accepted my apology, but I learned an important lesson: never use your prophetic authority and power when you are angry or offended by someone. That is when prophetic ministry can stop being life-giving and actually do damage. New Testament prophetic ministry is primarily for encouraging, strengthening and comforting people and never for bullying.

One woman told me about a traumatic experience. People declared over her in front of an entire church she was a failure in life and she would never succeed. Those people spoke a curse over her life. I immediately broke the power of those words by praying God's blessings over her. Life and death are in the power of our tongue, and prophecy should not be used to curse someone (see Prov. 18:21).

Charismatic Witchcraft

In 1 Samuel 18:10-11, we find a very odd story. Saul is "prophesying in his house" (NIV) when an evil spirit comes upon him. He takes his spear and tries to murder David by pinning him against a wall. Saul had learned how to prophesy by being around Samuel and the group of prophets. However, he was prophesying from a different spirit than the Holy Spirit. When this happens, the results can be deadly.

One woman came to Bible teacher Kenneth Hagin and complained about a group spending a lot of time prophesying over each other and only telling her bad things. They said her mom was going to die in six months. Eighteen months later, she was still alive. They also said her unbelieving husband was going to leave her. This was something she did not want. Hagin immediately released her from the negative words spoken over her.[13]

If someone does this, then it is most likely not the Holy Spirit leading them, but it is their own spirit, or possibly an evil spirit. We must use God's words to give life, otherwise we could fall into "charismatic witchcraft." This is not a woman with a long nose and a pointy hat riding a broomstick. Witchcraft is trying to intimidate, manipulate and control others. Misusing a word from God can do this. There are people who judge or curse other people or congregations. The fruit of such a ministry can be highly destructive, and it is distinctly ungodly.

When someone declares "God says" to promote their own political, social, personal, or church agenda, they may be shutting down all discussion. People should be free to share what they feel God is saying, but there should also be room for discussion and feedback to see if God is speaking to other people in the same line. Every prophetic word must be tested (see 1 Cor. 14:29).

Paul writes to the believers in Galatia saying, "O foolish Galatians! Who has bewitched you?" (Gal. 3:1). The people bewitching the Gentile believers were Jewish believers trying to force them to be circumcised in order to be saved. This was contrary to the spirit and message of Jesus that Paul had preached to the Galatians.

We must test every prophetic word and discern what spirit is motivating the person who is speaking. As John the beloved wrote, "Beloved, do not believe every spirit, but test the spirits to see whether they are from God, for many false prophets have gone out into the world" (1 John 4:1). Jesus warns of false prophets when He says, "Beware of false prophets, who come to you in sheep's clothing but inwardly are ravenous wolves. You will recognize them by their fruits" (Matt. 7:15-16).

I have had some experiences dealing with false prophets who are wolves in sheep's clothing. This type of people will not submit to any kind of leadership. They are full of rebellion and misuse God's name to promote their own agenda. To deceive the minds of gullible people they may use "smooth talk and flattery" (see Rom. 16:17-18). Such people will claim they can experience God's leading and claim anyone who disagrees is not hearing God. Pride, arrogance and insecurity hide behind their mask of "super-spirituality," and they can be very unstable and dangerous. It cannot be said often enough: every prophetic word must be tested! There are false prophets, but there are also real prophets. There are false teachers and pastors, but there are authentic ones as well. Do not allow the false to cause you to reject what is really from God.

My heart's desire is to see a new generation of prophets who are life-giving and building up individuals and churches. This is why guidelines must be followed and everyone involved must remain humble to avoid unnecessary casualties of prophetic ministry. We are not to despise prophecy, nor are we to discourage those who are trying to grow in hearing God's voice. We have to "hold on to what is good" and "reject every kind of evil" (see 1 Thess. 5:19-22 NIV). We should try to evaluate and judge every prophetic word. If someone gives you a word from God, test it. Realize that even the disciples, Peter, James and John, had moments in their ministry when they were not following the Holy Spirit and had to be rebuked by Jesus (see Matt. 16:23; Luke 9:54-55). If they could make mistakes, so can we!

I enjoy helping Christians grow in the prophetic. For example, one woman when first starting to prophesy would feel all the emotions of people she was prophesying to and tell them things about themselves that were neither strengthening, encouraging, nor comforting. I had to gently correct and encourage her. Now I am happy to see her flourish in her gift. She is not only operating in prophetic ministry biblically, she is activating others to do the same. No matter how much experience a person may have, there is always room for learning more and growing deeper in prophetic ministry.

There are definitely times when God can use someone to bring words of warning and correction to an individual or a church. However, these words must bring hope and life. In Revelation 2 and 3, Jesus brings words of correction to seven churches in Asia Minor. All of these words are woven in together with words of encouragement and promises of the rewards God has for them if they obey Him. Prophetic ministry should never bring condemnation or death to individuals but should bring hope and life even if there are words of correction involved.

As parents of our children, we regularly bring correction to them in the context of a deep, loving relationship. Nobody else can correct my children as my wife and I can because no one else loves them like we do. Correcting other people's children is not always good or effective because of a lack of relationship. Discipline without a relationship can lead to rebellion. This is why focusing on the most basic form of prophetic ministry (strengthening, encouraging and comforting) is best for everyone desiring to grow in this vital ministry.

Misunderstanding What Prophecy Is

Prophecy is not just *foretelling* the future, but also *forthtelling* what God thinks about a person or situation. Prophecy that is predictive is *foretelling*. Prophecy declares the thoughts and intentions of God's heart and the revelation of His will for a situation, a person, a place, or a situation—known as *forthtelling*.[14] People might not recognize the latter as prophecy, or they may feel so intimidated by foretelling they don't dare to simply pray and proclaim what God thinks and feels about an individual. They are blocked by a narrow definition of prophecy.

Forthtelling can be very similar to preaching. In fact, the first Protestant manual on preaching written in 1592 by William Perkins was called *The Art of Prophesying*. Prophesying is communicating God's heart and mind through our words and deeds. God can speak about the present, past, or future. There are different levels of prophetic ministry, and though not every believer is a prophet, every believer can learn to hear the voice of God and speak His words. Every believer can and should encourage, strengthen and comfort one another with words from God (see 1 Cor. 14:3). Prophecy has everything to do with knowing and connecting to God's heart. Every true prophetic word will then line up with His written Word in Scripture.

Being able to experience God's voice and power is truly life-changing, for you and for the people you get in touch with. Everything changes when prayer is no longer a religious obligation, but a two-way conversation with God. He is always speaking in many ways. It is wonderful to learn how we can connect with Him daily.

Prophecy in Scripture has to do with knowing and seeing God. Proverbs 29:18 says God's people perish because of a lack of revelation or prophetic vision. One Dutch version actually translates Proverbs 29:18 as, "God's people perish because of a lack of prophecy" (NBV). Obviously, God's people are not perishing because they are not foretelling the future—they are perishing because they know *about* God, but they don't know Him. As Hosea 4:6 says, "My people are being destroyed because they don't know me" (NLT).

Prophecy in the broadest sense is simply hearing, seeing, sensing and knowing God and then at times telling others what we have heard and seen from Jesus (see Rev. 19:10). Prophecy is a normal part of developing a healthy prayer life. We talk to God, and He talks to us. Hearing the voice of God and speaking his words (prophecy) should be normal for every believer.

Cessationism and Fear

> What father among you, if his son asks for a fish, will instead of a fish give him a serpent; or if he asks for an egg, will give him a scorpion? If you then, who are evil, know how to give good gifts to your children, how much more will the heavenly Father give the Holy Spirit to those who ask him!
> – LUKE 11:11-13

I remember one time, I was teaching some teenagers about the Holy Spirit. When I used the words "Holy Spirit," they started talking about ghosts and things they were afraid of. I knew treating the Holy Spirit this way would make them incapable of flowing in His gifts, so I showed them the Holy Spirit only gives *good* gifts. We never have to fear anything which truly comes from the Holy Spirit. Among His assignments on earth, the Holy Spirit came to comfort us, to teach us and to empower us (see John 14:16, 26; Acts 1:8).

A young person told me none of Paul's letters mention anything supernatural. He said that proved miracles, signs and wonders are no longer for today. I then showed him entire chapters in Paul's epistles which instruct us to grow in the gifts of the Holy Spirit and use signs and wonders to share our faith. He had been taught God does not do anything supernatural because we have the Bible. This false teaching is called cessationism. It is based on people's experience of never seeing God do something supernatural. It is incorrect to create a teaching based on our experience and not upon what the Bible really teaches. Nowhere in Scripture does it say God has ceased speaking and healing the sick.

Cessationism is based on a misinterpretation of a scripture which is ironically in the middle of Paul's teaching of how we should desire and grow in spiritual gifts. This is the scripture that is misinterpreted:

Love never fails. But where there are prophecies, they will cease; where there are tongues, they will be stilled; where there is knowledge, it will pass away. For we know in part and we prophesy in part, but when completeness comes, what is in part disappears. When I was a child, I talked like a child, I thought like a child, I reasoned like a child. When I became a man, I put the ways of childhood behind me.
– 1 CORINTHIANS 13:8-11 (NIV)

It says what is in part like prophecy, tongues and knowledge, will cease when completion comes. Cessationism states that the Holy Bible is completely and perfectly the Word of God and we no longer need any gifts of the Spirit. One woman told me I was a liar when I told her about healing because according to her this scripture states that after the time of the apostles God stopped healing people and using any spiritual gifts.

This misinterpretation of Scripture totally takes chapter 13 out of context of chapters 12 and 14, which repeatedly tell us to pursue spiritual gifts, especially the gift of prophecy. Jesus said that all believers could lay their hands on the sick and heal them (Mark 16:18) and that we should heal the sick when sharing the gospel of the kingdom (Matt. 10:8). "When completeness comes" (NIV) is definitely not speaking of the closed canon of the Bible. It is speaking of when Jesus returns and we will all become just like Him (1 John 3:2).

When we see Jesus fully, we will not need prophecy, healing, words of knowledge and tongues. In the meantime, we are living in a world which needs to hear words from God and experience his healing. God has not stopped and will not stop speaking and healing this world. We are privileged to have the written Word of God, but it does not replace the need for people to experience God now. Having said that, our experience never supersedes the written Word of God. Everything is under the authority of Scripture. Scripture gives us the protection and covering we need to process experiences which may have come from the Holy Spirit. For example, my heart was broken once when an unmarried couple told me it was okay to have sex with each other because the Holy Spirit said it was alright. They were definitely not listening to the Holy Spirit, as sex outside of marriage is explicitly forbidden in Scripture.

Moving in the gifts of the Holy Spirit require us to be tethered to Scripture. History is littered with examples of false prophets such as Joseph Smith who supposedly saw an angel along with golden tablets and created a new religion called Mormonism. His gospel is very different from what the Bible teaches. Paul warns the Galatians: "But even if we or an angel from heaven should preach to you a gospel contrary to the one we preached to you, let him be accursed" (Gal. 1:8). Prophecy is never meant to create new doctrines and teaching that are against Scripture.

Many churches claim to be trinitarian; they believe in the Father, the Son and the Holy Spirit. In reality they are binarian, because the Holy Spirit is kept out of their daily lives. And yet they claim they are based on the Bible! Their creed should say, "We believe in the Father, the Son and the Holy Scriptures!" The Holy Spirit is seen as an old, scary uncle who may show up at family gatherings and no one knows what to do with him. People may fear things done in the name of the Holy Spirit due to stories of abuses and false teachings. They throw away the baby with the dirty bathwater. Please do not get rid of spiritual gifts because of abuses and excesses.

Driving a car can be dangerous. Yet we still drive cars, in a safe way. The gifts of the Holy Spirit used in an incorrect manner can be disruptive and dangerous. So, we need to learn how to use them in a safe manner. As Paul said, "So, my brothers, earnestly desire to prophesy, and do not forbid speaking in tongues. But all things should be done decently and in order" (1 Cor. 14:39-40). Each of us has the ability to walk in the gifts of the Spirit in a way that is life-giving and orderly when we do so regularly, lovingly and humbly.

Other Prerequisites Than Faith

We do not have to work up our emotions, feel the anointing, speak in King James English, or fall into a trance in order to prophesy. All gifts from God—including salvation, healing, tongues, words of knowledge and prophecy—work by faith (see Eph. 2:8-9).

We may be speaking the very words of God, but we don't have to be weird doing it. We are to speak trusting God will inspire our words (see 1 Pet. 4:11). Simply begin by praying for people in a way which strengthens, encourages and comforts them. *Everyone* can prophesy at this basic level.

One leader of a large Pentecostal church told me he could only prophesy at the end of meetings. This is when he could *feel* the anointing and his faith was high. Yet the Bible says we operate by faith, and not by what we see or feel (see 2 Cor. 5:7). We can open our mouths and trust God to fill them (see

Ps. 81:10). When we open our mouths, prophecy may start as a small trickle from a faucet, but as we continue it may begin to flow like a river.

The evangelist Smith Wigglesworth was once at a church meeting where, after sitting in prayer quietly, he began speaking God's words fluently and easily as if liquid fire was flowing from his lips. The leaders at the end of the service remarked, "How quickly you are moved by the Spirit! What is your secret? Do please tell us." They were somewhat astounded at his blunt reply, "Well, you see, it is like this. If the Spirit does not move me, I move the Spirit."[15] Paul said the "spirits of prophets are subject to the control of prophets" (see 1 Cor. 14:32 NIV). This means we are the ones who initiate prophecy. If we wait for God to come and force our tongue to move, we will never speak. If you say you believe in prophecy and never prophecy, you probably don't believe you can. Belief without actions is dead (see James 5:17). What a person does shows what they truly believe and not only what they say.

To move in the Spirit, we do not need an angel to sit on our head or any supernatural manifestations to take place. Wigglesworth once said, "I am not moved by what I feel. I am not moved by what I see. I am moved only by what I believe. I cannot understand God by feelings. I understand God by what the Word says about Him."[16]

Through faith in God and His Word, we can prophesy. The Bible instructs us to "be eager to prophesy" (1 Cor. 14:39 NIV;

see Matt. 10:8). We do not have to wait for a feeling or sign. We simply step out and begin speaking while trusting our heavenly Father to, together with us, take the wheel. It is easier to steer a moving car than a stopped one. Open your mouth and trust God to fill it. Trust that if you ask God for bread, He will not give you a stone. Trust Him that He can speak through you.

Fear of Making a Mistake

When my son began walking, I did not tell him he could not walk when he repeatedly fell down. Instead, I encouraged him to continue trying to walk until he could. Often churches do not create a safe place where people can grow in prophetic ministry without being shut down if they do make a mistake. If you want to grow in prophecy you have to have faith, and faith is spelled R-I-S-K. Whenever I prophesy, I am taking a risk. I am telling someone things about their lives and what God thinks of them without knowing anything about them. I become vulnerable. I am aware I can make a mistake and look stupid. Learning to prophesy is rather like learning to speak a new language.

When I first came to Holland, I could not speak very much Dutch. All I could say in Dutch was: "Hello, my name is Matt. I really want to learn Dutch. This is all that I know. Can you help me? Thank you very much. Goodbye."

I repeated this phrase literally to hundreds of people. Femke did not like talking to me in Dutch during the first six months of living here because it was like talking to a little child. However, I persevered and now I can preach and teach fluently, although not perfectly, in Dutch. Paul also says that when we prophesy, we do it in part (1 Cor. 13:9). We do not know everything, we simply share what we see or hear God saying. The more we do it, the more fluent we will be in prophesying.

In Amsterdam, there are people who only speak English. This is because English is understood in most parts of my city. Because they are afraid of looking stupid or have not invested the time and energy to learn Dutch, they don't speak it, and avoid sounding like an ignorant child. But most Dutch speakers will appreciate someone trying to learn Dutch, and with enough practice they may become fluent someday.

In the same way, if you want to grow strong in prophecy, you need to overcome your fear of making a mistake. Remember the goal of prophecy is showing God's love and truth to people. Am I willing to look stupid in order to prophesy? Was I willing to look stupid in order to learn Dutch? You better believe it.

If I were to stop speaking in Dutch, I would lose it. If you quit prophesying, you can also considerably weaken your prophetic muscle. Some people I have trained in prophetic ministry stop prophesying once I leave. Others continue prophesying and become strong in prophetic ministry because they are not dependent on my presence for them to prophesy. They have learned to depend on the Holy Spirit in them to prophesy and not on me. The same Holy Spirit I have, they do too.

I have seen how prophecy can build people up and change lives. My desire to prophesy is greater than my fear of making a mistake. As long as you desire to strengthen, encourage and comfort people with words from God you will most likely do more good than harm. Don't let your fear of making a mistake keep you from prophesying.

When the Barriers Are Overcome

Any parent would be disappointed to find all the Christmas and birthday presents they bought for a child stored up in a closet having never been touched by their child. God has many "spiritual" gifts for his children to use but they are not being opened and played with. The gifts of the Holy Spirit are for all His children, and as John Wimber used to say, "Everyone gets to play." Everybody can prophesy, heal the sick, get a word of knowledge, cast out demons, et cetera (see Mark 16:15-18). By overcoming the barriers, we do what God wants us to do.

The gifts of the Holy Spirit are *gifts*. They do not depend on us earning points or being "good." They are given to us by grace, which we receive and use by faith (see Eph. 2:8-9). We prophesy because God loves to speak to people through us.

As I developed this gift, I learned to love to prophesy whenever I can and as often as possible. I love to receive a word or picture from the Lord for my life and for the lives of others. We do not have to work up emotions or feel something special to prophesy. We can open our mouths by faith and deliver a life-giving word from God to someone. Just do it!

If one hundred people stand before me, I can trust that God will enable me to prophesy over all of them. However, I would rather train five other people so we could all serve twenty individuals. Like Samuel and Elijah, I am passionate about training up schools or groups of believers who can prophesy. You can also hear God's voice and speak His words. You can prophesy! What is hindering you?

PROPHESY—*JUST DO IT!*

EXERCISE 1
Use God's Word as a Hammer (individual)

Atheism, deism, individualism, rationalism, materialism, and cessationism are some of the barriers to prophetic ministry. Take time to study and see what the Bible says about them and use God's Word as a hammer shattering these ideas (Jer. 23:29).

Atheism and deism: Atheism says God does not exist. Deism says he exists, but he is not involved in our daily lives. Read: Matt. 6:25-34; 10:29-30; 28:16-20; Luke 11:9-13; Rom. 8:14-17; 1 John 3:1; Ps. 139; Jer. 31:3; 33:3.

Individualism: This teaches the individual is the most important. I must believe and do what I want and it does not matter what others want or think. Read: Rom. 8:5-13; 1 Cor. 12:12-26; Gal. 5:13-26; Eph. 2:1-6.

Rationalism: The belief we must rationally understand everything to be able to accept it. Read: Eph. 3:14-21; Phil. 4:3-7; Job 36:26; Ps. 147:5; Prov. 3:5-6.

Materialism: This idea teaches only what we can experience with our five senses is real. Read: Matt. 6:19-20; 16:16; 24:35; Luke 12:15; 1 Tim. 6:17; Eccles. 5:15.

Cessationism: This holds that God stopped using Spiritual Gifts such as prophecy, healing, and tongues after we received the Holy Bible. Read: Matt. 10:7-8; 28:16-20; Mark 16:15-19; Luke 12:11-12; John 14:12; Rom. 15:14-20; 1 Cor. 2:1-6, 12-14; 1 Thess. 5:19-21; 1 Tim. 1:18; 4:13-14; 2 Tim. 1:6-7.

EXERCISE 2
One Word (group)

What impedes people from prophesying, praying for healing, speaking in tongues, etc.? We think too much. We do not prophesy from our own thoughts, but from our spirit. This exercise enables people to relax and release one word, trusting God to speak through whatever we may say.

Everyone in the group has a pen and a paper to write down the words given to them. Then everyone gives each person in the group one word. At the end of the exercises, every person will have a list of words with which they can use to begin deciphering God's word to them. Use three steps: revelation, interpretation and application.

This exercise helps participants relax and learn to prophesy from their spirit and not from their own thinking. The more one learns to tap into God's Spirit, the more one can begin to discern which thoughts are from God, and which are one's own.

Also, once everyone has their list together, have them swap lists with a neighbor and, using each other's list, prophesy over each other. For example, if the first three words are life, banana and joy, I could prophesy something like, "I am filling you today with My life and know your words are like delicious bananas which give many people much strength. I have great joy in you and My joy will be your strength."

Do the same with all the words on your neighbor's paper and then have them prophesy over you using the words on your paper. Don't worry about having deep or impacting words, at this level; just focus on strengthening, encouraging and comforting each other with the words on the sheet of paper. At times, I have looked at a person and said a name of a relative or loved one. Other times it is simply a word such as "love" or "power." Do not judge a word by how deep or simple it may be.

Kris Vallotton tells of a man telling a woman, "You have a yellow shirt on!" The woman wasn't actually wearing a yellow shirt at all. The woman started weeping hysterically. When asked why she reacted so, she explained, "I have a son who is autistic, and I told the Lord today, 'If You are going to heal my son, have someone tell me I have on a yellow shirt.'"[17]

EXERCISE 3
Around the Circle (group)

Everyone get in one circle (or in a number of circles of four to five people if you are in a large group). Everyone in the circle will prophesy over the person on their right until everyone in the group has prophesied over the person next to them. When first beginning, students may be afraid to speak. Encourage them to simply pray words of encouragement, strengthening and comfort. This is the most basic form of prophetic ministry.

This is normally the first exercise I do with people to "warm up." Because the word "prophecy" holds so much weight in their mind, it can be difficult for them to speak. Encourage them to simply pray for each other. Prophecy is a natural part of prayer because when we speak to God, He will speak back to us.

EXERCISE 4
Switch (group)

The group leader will say "switch" when people need to stop or start prophesying. This is actually a tool to be used in all of the other group exercises. If they say "switch" quickly, this will force participants to not think too much but simply by faith say what the Spirit of God will lead them to say. If the switch is delayed, this will challenge those prophesying to not stop prophesying, but by faith ask God for more they can give. A prophet is in control of themselves and can be quiet when they need to be quiet, such as when it is not their turn to speak.

One woman who traveled with me had a difficult time with me calling "switch" while she was prophesying the first time. She wanted to give the entire message God had for a person at that moment. Through this exercise she learned the value of being able to hold onto a word from God. Just because God may give you a word for someone does not mean you have to give the entire word at that moment. Learning to wait for the right timing is important. It is also important to learn to submit to authority when they feel it is not the right moment to give a word or pray.

On a trip to a youth conference in Ukraine, I had a ministry team wanting to go pray for healing. I told them, however, to wait. My team trusted me, and later they understood why it was not yet time for us to pray for the sick. Instead of us doing all the praying, I wanted to get the Ukrainian students praying for the sick and see healings take place. I wanted to first equip others so they would be dependent on God and not on us.

EXERCISE 5
All on One (group)

One person stands in the middle of the group, and everyone in the group prophesies one by one over that person. Everyone else shares what they feel God may be saying. This is a great exercise to build up one person. I have seen the person in the middle extremely impacted by the prophetic words released over their lives during this exercise. Many people are not used to being strengthened, encouraged and comforted by others. Expressing God's love is powerful.

EXERCISE 6

One on All (group)

One person stands in the middle of the group and will prophesy over everyone in the group. This exercise gets a person outside of their comfort zone. They do not have time to think but have to prophesy over the next person totally by faith. Whatever picture, scripture, or feeling comes up, they must communicate that in a way that is strengthening, encouraging and comforting. This person's faith will be built up as they realize they can prophesy over many people by faith.

CHAPTER 4

Prophecy in the Church

Prophetic ministry can be intentionally cultivated and developed to serve the local church and the world. To develop it, though, the different levels of prophetic ministry need to be understood. These different levels can be compared to the different depths of a swimming pool. Allow me to explain. Rearing my children in the Netherlands requires them to take swimming lessons, as there are many bodies of water they may fall into. This is a rite of passage in the Netherlands, and my children all have their swimming diplomas. They can dive, go through underwater obstacles and swim fearlessly at the deep end of the pool. They have all completed courses in swimming, something I never did. When I was six years old, I deliberately landed on my swimming teacher when I jumped off the diving board. I was afraid of swimming at the deep end! I much preferred to stay at the shallow end, where I could reach the bottom of the pool. Just as swimming at the shallow end of the pool is significantly different from swimming at the deep end, there are differences in prophesying at the different levels of the prophetic ministry. For our purposes, I want to define the shallow end as the spirit of prophecy, where everyone can jump in. I will define the middle area as the gift of prophecy, where many may be able to prophesy, and the deep end as the office of the prophet, where fewer people are called and equipped to function.

THE OFFICE OF THE PROPHET
FEW BECOME PROPHETS

THE GIFT OF PROPHECY
MANY MAY HAVE THIS GIFT

THE SPIRIT OF PROPHECY
ALL MAY PROPHESY

In his book, *Growing in the Prophetic*, Mike Bickle has a diagram which helps illustrate this point.[18] On the left side of the diagram,

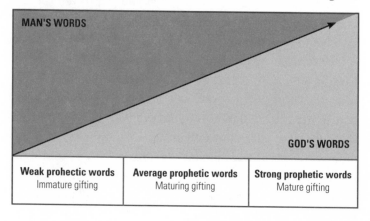

MAN'S WORDS

GOD'S WORDS

Weak prohectic words	Average prophetic words	Strong prophetic words
Immature gifting	Maturing gifting	Mature gifting

the simplest form of prophetic ministry is illustrated. There, a high percentage of what is said may simply be coming from a person's own heart mixed in with some words that come from God. As a person grows in prophetic ministry and intimacy with God, the percentage of accurate words from God continues to increase and words that are simply from their own heart decreases. Prophecy at this third level is most purely from God. Nevertheless, even the most experienced prophet can deliver a prophetic word that comes from their own heart and not from God's heart. This is why testing words and giving feedback to those who desire to grow in prophetic ministry is so vital (see 1 Thess. 5:19-22).

One Saturday morning, one of my children came to me and said, "Papa, Mama wants you to go to the bakery and buy croissants and warm bread for breakfast." I immediately knew these were the words that came from my Femke. She likes to have bread from the bakery on Saturday mornings. My child proceeded to say, "And she says she wants there to be cheese croissants and chocolate croissants." I realized my child was misusing the name of my wife to get what my child desired. My child wanted the cheese and the chocolate croissants, but I know my wife never wants that.

In the same way, we must listen to words given to us and discern what is coming from God's heart and what can be simply coming from the person's own desire or opinion. Discernment and wisdom are necessary when evaluating a prophetic word. If we have a personal relationship with God, then we can have a pretty good idea when a word truly comes from Him and not from someone's own heart. Just like I know Femke well enough to recognize her words in my children's words, so can we know God well enough to recognize His words in the words of His children. There is responsibility on the part of the individuals who prophesy, but also on the part of those who receive a prophetic word. They should test the prophetic message and decide in prayer what they think God says.

One day a leader called to inform me a pastor had been telling everyone I had prophesied some people out of his church. I immediately called this leader to ask him what had happened. I had met some people from his church who had taken the prophetic word I gave them to mean they were supposed to leave their home church. The problem is I would never tell someone (especially someone I do not know at all) they should leave their home church. This was their interpretation. I asked the pastor if he had listened to the recording of the prophetic word I gave. He had not and apologized for simply taking what they said and not really hearing what I had actually said. This highlights the importance of recording prophetic words when possible.

We must be careful not to spread gossip and misinformation about people, especially if we have only heard things through the gossip grapevine. Life and death are in the power of the tongue, as Proverbs 18:21 tells us, and often many ministries suffer from being unfairly criticized and judged by other believers. If you have not heard or seen something first-hand, think before you start talking and spreading lies. Then we are definitely more like Satan, "the father of lies" (John 8:44) than Jesus.

Shawn Bolz in his book *Translating God* tells of seasoned and experienced prophets who nearly always prophesy accurately, but when they prophesied about certain subjects their words were nearly always inaccurate. This had to do with those prophets' own need for inner healing or their own opinions.[19] People can mistake things which simply come from their own hearts and are not necessarily coming from God's heart. This highlights the need for accountability and transparency for *everyone* who ministers and receive God's Word.

Let's take a step back and examine each level of prophecy in turn. Let us start at the shallow end of the prophetic swimming pool, the Spirit of Prophecy.

The Spirit of Prophecy

The Spirit of Prophecy is the entry level of prophetic ministry. Revelation 19:10 says, "'Worship God.' For the testimony of Jesus is the spirit of prophecy." In the Old Testament, an example of this is found in 1 Samuel:

> Then Saul sent messengers to take David, and when they saw the company of the prophets prophesying, and Samuel standing as head over them, the Spirit of God came upon the messengers of Saul, and they also

> prophesied. When it was told Saul, he sent other messengers, and they
> also prophesied. And Saul sent messengers again the third time, and
> they also prophesied. Then he himself went to Ramah ... And the Spirit
> of God came upon him also, and as he went he prophesied until he came
> to Naioth in Ramah. And he too stripped off his clothes, and he too
> prophesied before Samuel and lay naked all that day and all that night.
> Thus, it is said, "Is Saul also among the prophets?"
> – 1 SAMUEL 19:20-24

Saul and his soldiers wanted to capture David, but instead, the Spirit of God overpowered them, and they all began to prophesy. This is a wonderful example of how even unbelievers can be prophesying under a strong anointing of the Spirit of Prophecy. The Spirit of Prophecy can show them God is real and His presence can actually be felt.

Once I spoke at a youth group where no one was interested at all in prophetic ministry. Early in the evening, one woman said she did not know if God really existed. Then I learned three of the young men there were Muslims. Faith and expectancy for God to move was nonexistent. This all changed when I began prophesying to them. Their eyes were wide open as I started telling them one by one about things in their past, present and future. For about an hour, I prophesied over each of them, and I could sense the level of their faith getting higher and higher. After that, I issued a challenge for each one to ask God to say something to them. To my amazement, all of them—including the agnostic woman and Muslim men—started receiving accurate words and mental pictures with symbolic meaning from God!

The highlight of the evening for me was seeing the change which took place in the woman who had said earlier she wanted to know if God really existed. Tears ran down her face as God spoke to and through her. A few weeks later, I baptized her.

A beautiful example of the power of prophecy in the Church is found in 1 Corinthians 14:

> But if *all prophesy*, and an unbeliever or outsider enters, he is convicted by all, he is called to account by all, the secrets of his heart are disclosed, and so, falling on his face, he will worship God and declare that *God is really among you.*
> – 1 CORINTHIANS 14:24-25

In no way am I advocating non-Christians or immature, rebellious Christians regularly prophesy. Those who wish to prophesy regularly must be accountable, humble and studying the Scriptures. All prophecies must be evaluated and tested by Scripture. If they contradict Scripture, do not accept them. This is important especially when the Spirit of Prophecy is strong, because *anyone* with a high level of faith can potentially prophesy. This Spirit of Prophecy, the shallow end of the prophetic swimming pool, thrives under specific circumstances:

1. During the time of worship when the Spirit of God is very tangible. All may easily receive a message from God.
2. When people come into a group of prophets or are chal lenged by a minister to jump in and start prophesying.[20]

At this level, all prophesying should be focused on strengthening, encouragement and comforting one another and *not* foretelling the future (see 1 Cor. 14:3). Prophetic messages at this level should not be corrective or directional and should aim at encouraging people and making the love of God tangible.

Avoid prophesying about births, marriages, healings or deaths in the shallow end. God does speak about these things, but it involves a higher level of responsibility, which is better left for the more experienced ministers or prophets. If God does reveal something regarding one of those issues, ask Him if you should say anything, and if so, when and to whom. If in doubt, refer to a mature leader as to what to say or do regarding such a word. If you do make a mistake in any of these areas, apologize.

For example, if God reveals someone is going to marry someone else, you could simply write it in a sealed and dated envelope, and on the day of the wedding you can give it to the newly married couple. In this way, you'll avoid making claims that reach beyond your prophetic development and causing unnecessary confusion.

Prophetic ministry has gotten a black eye in the past because people misuse a "word from God" to manipulate people and force them to do things they do not necessarily desire. Having guidelines and accountability to other ministers and prophets helps protect and cultivate a healthy, life-giving prophetic culture.

The Gift of Prophecy

The Gift of Prophecy is one of the nine gifts of the Holy Spirit that the apostle Paul describes in 1 Corinthians 12:4-11. Those who realize they have this gift may use it anywhere and everywhere by faith. For me, it makes little difference if I am at a church, a supermarket, a street corner, a business office, a brothel, or even at a psychic fair: by faith I can prophesy because I know God is always speaking. Romans 12:6 says, "If God has given you the ability to prophesy, then prophesy whenever you can—as often as your faith is strong enough to receive a message from God" (TLB). This means I always try to keep my faith strong and my "spiritual antennas" ready, so at any moment I can receive and deliver a message from God.

When I first started moving in the prophetic in 2010, I inquired of a prophet in Tulsa how to do prophetic evangelism. I asked her, "Do I ask for a clue? Do I go treasure hunting?" She replied, "No, you just have the guts to walk up to someone and tell them what God wants to tell them." So that night I went to a drugstore and two gas stations where I walked up to strangers and told them what God wanted to tell them. It was and still remains something which takes a lot of courage, but I find I get a huge rush when I get to deliver an accurate word of knowledge or a prophetic word to an absolute stranger on the street.

Kenneth Hagin describes a prophet as someone who operates not only in the gift of prophecy, but also regularly and strongly has two or three other gifts of the Spirit functioning in their life.[21] At least three or four of the gifts of the Holy Spirit regularly manifest in my life. I can pray in the Spirit, pray for the sick, prophesy and interpret tongues by faith nearly at any moment and in any place. The gifts of the Spirit are much like the rings in the Olympic flag: they are connected and merge into each other. I can easily be speaking in tongues and then get a word of knowledge. That may lead to praying for healing which can lead back to prophetic ministry. Some leaders like to differentiate when someone is using which gift. But to be honest I don't necessarily know if what I am saying is a word of knowledge or a prophetic word.

For example, I was in Budapest prophesying over a leader that he would bring great resources and finances into the local church. My interpreter stopped me and said, "That is a word of knowledge. He does that already."

"Oh... okay," I replied. "And he will keep doing it."

One young developing prophet wrote me and asked me why he was suddenly knowing that people were dealing with fear and thoughts of suicide. I responded that he was starting to get words of knowledge and discernment of spirits. When people get activated in prophetic ministry, it is quite normal for the other gifts to begin operating in their lives as well. All nine gifts of the Holy Spirit have manifested in my life at different times and in different measures, yet there are three or four which seem to be the strongest. I desire to continue growing in these, but also growing in other gifts of the Spirit to better be able to serve the body of Christ.

The way to find out if someone has a gift of prophecy is by listening to people prophesy while doing prophetic exercises. Sometimes individuals will stick out as you listen to them prophesy over you and others. The more people practice, the more they may develop this gift. Listen to them and listen to what you feel the Lord may be saying about them, because some individuals may be called to not only have a gift of prophecy but called to the highest level of prophetic ministry: the office of the prophet.

The Office of the Prophet

> And he gave the apostles, the prophets, the evangelists, the shepherds and teachers, to equip the saints for the work of ministry, for building up the body of Christ.
> – EPHESIANS 4:11-12a

> Surely the LORD God does nothing, Unless He reveals His secret to His
> servants the prophets.
> – AMOS 3:7 (NKJV)

The office of the prophet is one of the five ministry gifts
Christ has given to the Church. He did this in order to equip
all believers to do the work of the ministry and to see them
develop lives of stability and maturity (see Eph. 4:11-14). Prophets
work together with apostles, pastors, evangelists and teachers
and should never work alone. Just as teachers teach people to
teach and evangelists help people to evangelize, so prophets
teach people how to discern God's voice and speak His words.

The primary ministry gifts the Church in the Western
world focuses on are those of the teacher and the pastor.
Therefore, there are many outstanding teachers and pastors,
but there are relatively few known prophets. We need prophets.
Prophets are a powerful and necessary gift to the body of
Christ. Prophets can help bring about real changes, including
miracles and spiritual breakthroughs, to individuals, churches,
whole communities and even nations. Their ministry often
involves miracles and spiritual breakthroughs.

Experienced and skilled prophets are not limited to
strengthening, encouraging and comforting people, but may
also operate in other areas such as giving of guidance, correction,
healing, creative miracles, prophetic worship and spiritual
warfare. There are even prophets changing weather patterns.

One example of a contemporary prophet (who does not refer to himself as a prophet) is Pastor Robert Morris from Gateway Church in Dallas, Texas. He has a huge amount of experience in prophetic ministry and tells stories such as when God told him his daughter was pregnant. The only problem was that she was medically unable to become pregnant. Nevertheless, she went to the doctor and started taking progesterone just in case she was pregnant (her progesterone levels were too low). Sure enough, she was pregnant and because of that word she and the baby were safe. A similar prophecy was given by a Mexican prophet and personal friend of mine, Beatriz Romero. While in Spain, she told a fifty-year-old woman that in nine months she was going to give birth to a healthy child. And it happened.

Just as there are many different kinds of teachers and pastors, so there are many different kinds of prophets with different styles and assignments. There are prophets who prophesy in a song, dance, painting or sermon. Other prophesy over individuals —businessmen or political leaders. Do not allow your preconceived ideas or stereotypes of what a prophet looks like impede you from seeing contemporary prophets. A real-life example illustrates how that works. When Benjamin was four years old, we lost track of him at a large lake. I went searching for a little boy with a large life jacket on. I saw a cute blonde boy playing by the water, but he did not have the life jacket on I was looking for. I kept looking for the life jacket. Shortly afterwards, my wife found Benjamin. It was the little cute blonde boy I had seen! He had taken off his life jacket and that impeded me from seeing his true identity.

Jesus once said a prophet is not recognized in his own town (see Luke 4:24). When people may be familiar with an individual, they may not be able to see the calling and gifting on their lives. The Nazarites could not fathom that Jesus was a powerful prophet, as they knew his entire family. Let's keep an open mind so we can recognize prophets. What is impeding you from seeing people God is calling to be a prophet? Often I have prophesied over individuals: "You are a prophet. Come prophesy." They are like eagles being allowed to soar when they begin powerfully and accurately prophesying. They are allowed to put on a prophet's mantle although they had no idea they could wear it.

We need to raise up a new generation of prophets who know how to work together with other leaders. That's how ministries *complete* each other. A prophet never usurps the authority of a pastor or local church leaders, but coordinates with them to edify the Church. Whenever I am ministering in a church, I make it clear I am under the authority of the leaders of that ministry. They have the right to give me feedback and correct me. A prophet's authority in a church is granted to them by its leadership – it cannot be usurped by the prophet. True prophets love people and build them up (see 1 Cor. 14:4-5). But of false prophets, the Bible says: "You have not gone up into the breaches, or built up a wall for the house of Israel, that it might stand in battle in the day of the LORD" (Ezek. 13:5).

Prophets are prayer warriors. When a warrior stood in a breach in a city's defensive wall, they were saying to the enemy forces, "You will only come into my city over my dead body." This is a role of the prophet: they stand in the gap and defend against the enemy.

Prayer is an essential element in the office of the prophet. The Dutch prophet Wim Kok has a busy family life with five children. Yet often when I call him he is praying. He loves nothing better than worshiping God and praying for people. I will never forget the time he kept waking me up every night during a trip we went on to Kiev. He was softly praying to God all night long. For him, prayer is the ultimate pleasure in life. Several seasoned prophets I know were at one time the pastors in charge of prayer ministry at their churches. They would spend hours a week praying. This prayer life is also why God can trust His prophets with His secrets, because they really are His friends (see Amos 3:7).

Prophets care for their communities, churches and cities. True prophets build up communities to create places where people can find safety, healing and strength to go through the difficulties of life. Prophets help God's people to achieve things they thought impossible. For example, Haggai and Zechariah motivated the Hebrews to rebuild the temple at a time when they thought it would be impossible (see Ezra 5:1-2).

Moses led the Israelites through the Red Sea (see Ex. 14:21). Jesus fed thousands of people with a few pieces of fish and bread. He raised others from the dead (see John 6:1-14; 11:43-44).

Growing up, I watched how prophets brought significant breakthroughs in the churches we helped start in the United States. The few prophets we knew had a significant impact in our lives and ministries. They were people who would spend hours at a time praying and had regular times of fasting. The way they grew in prophetic ministry was spending time in God's presence. Spending quality time in prayer is vital and important, but prophets can also be mentored and trained in order to accelerate this growth process. Graham Cooke, in his book *Developing Your Prophetic Gifting*,[22] states that it normally takes an individual around twenty years to become mature as a prophet, but this time can be reduced to twelve years if they receive prophetic mentoring and training.

Making Room for Prophecy in the Church

For the leaders reading this book who wonder, "What should I do about prophets in my local church?" let me give you some advice.

First, read Scripture and as many books as possible describing scripturally sound contemporary prophecy. Second, find someone who has a flourishing biblical prophetic ministry. In the Netherlands, it is easier to find strong prophetic ministries than ten or twenty years ago. Third, have someone who can effectively teach, demonstrate and activate you and your church leaders to prophesy. Fourth, realize there probably are already people in your church who have a strong prophetic gifting. They may even be called to someday become prophets. One of those individuals might be you. However, without intentionally developing this area it is less likely it will develop in your church.

Finally, lead the change. Realize, however, that you do not need a prophet to develop prophetic ministry in your church. The prophetic is actually not about prophetic ministry; it is about knowing and listening to Jesus. Everyone can grow in their sensitivity and ability to hear God's voice. Prophetic ministry is not for only a few chosen individuals, but for all believers. That's why I teach schools of prophecy. Some churches have experienced little lasting fruit, others experience radical change. The difference between those two is leadership in the church. Those churches where the leaders began prophesying and healing the sick, their churches often followed. Prophets are also flesh and blood and should never be placed on a pedestal. Neither the prophets in the Bible nor present-day prophets are infallible. Prophets have need of friends who care about them as individuals and not simply because of God's calling on their lives. Prophets are also not always aware of the impact of their words.

One day, I was at a barbecue in Tulsa, Oklahoma. I walked up to a man and asked him if I could pray for him. He said,

"Sure." I then began describing him as a businessman and telling him all about the business he was contemplating beginning. I told him about medical equipment he was going to sell. I told him I felt that God said, "Go for it, now is the time."

Later, I found out that Tim had given up his business to become the worship leader at a local church in Tulsa. One day, his wife, a nurse, complained about the difficulties her patients had with their plastic tubes when they were undergoing oxygen treatment. Tim got an idea. He developed a remote control that helped the patients roll up their oxygen hoses. He started researching it and talking to businesspeople who could help him set up the financing. He also made a prototype.

That weekend he was waiting on God to give him a confirmation about whether he should take a second mortgage on his home and invest in this invention. Then I walked up to him and gave him that prophetic word. This is how he describes it:

> After you finished, I remember looking at you with amazement and I asked you seriously, "Have you spoken to my wife?" To which you laughed and replied, "Brother, I don't know you from Adam. I have definitely not spoken to your wife." I just couldn't believe the specificity with which you spoke into my life. I then talked to my wife and we went for it! We took out the loan and continued to develop the device. Almost three years later, we have filed two patents. We only brought the device to

market July of 2017 and have sold over five hundred units all over the world. We haven't even advertised yet, we only have a website and a Facebook page. Our customers are so grateful! People who aren't on oxygen cannot realize the degree of suffering being attached to a long, unmanageable tube adds to a person's life.

We are discussing the next step with two godly men who are interested in investing in our company. Although the Lord blesses us abundantly, this has been a difficult journey. We are facing a mountain of debt, and although we have sold so many units, we have reinvested nearly every dollar back into the business. Obviously, there is no turning back for us now! I fully believe the Lord has led us into this desert and He will bring us through into a good place. This company and this device will be a blessing for the world, like you prophesized. My wife and I live simply; our lives and all that we have will be poured out for the kingdom of God. We are so grateful you were obedient to God and gave me that word.

Tim's story is not yet finished, but neither is ours. Perhaps God is not calling you to become a prophet, but He is calling all of us to prophesy. In the next chapter I want to share a simple key which will enable you to grow in prophecy.

PROPHESY—*JUST DO IT!*

EXERCISE 1
Prophesy Over a Whole Group (group)
Sometimes you will have an opportunity to prophesy over an entire group. Prophets in the Bible prophesied over entire cities and

nations. For this exercise, deliver a word that applies to everyone present. Speak to them what God wants to say to them as a group. When prophesying over a whole group or church, just see them as one person and speak as if they were one.

Popcorn Prophecy (group)

When you have a large group of people and a limited amount of time, you need to be able to give a short word to each person and keep going on. It does not need to be a long word for it to be powerful. If you have a large group, go quickly and give each person a short prophetic blast of fifteen to twenty seconds. This exercise is good to get you out of leaning on your own thinking and trusting God that when you open your mouth He will speak.

Interpret a Dream (group)

Interpretations and the true meaning of dreams come from God (see Gen. 40:8). Have someone share a dream they had and ask God what it means. Share what you think God is saying.

Interpret a Name (individual)

Your name is not given to you by accident. Research the meaning of your name. Ask God what your name or names say about your true identity.

EXERCISE 5
The Blind Prophet (group)
The easiest way to prophesy is when you don't know over whom you are prophesying. Then you simply say what you feel and see. This exercise can be done just like the exercise "One on All" except that the person prophesying has their eyes closed. Have someone else in the group point at the person the blind prophet is prophesying over. Have the prophet also prophesy over themselves without knowing it. My favorite prophecies are words that I have given over myself without even knowing I was prophesying over myself. Be sure to have someone record your prophecy when you prophesy over yourself so you can hear it later.

EXERCISE 6
Prophesy Over Yourself (individual)
The most difficult persons to prophesy over are people that you know very well, such as your children or your spouse. Prophesying over yourself is also very difficult. Nevertheless, you should practice this. Grab a voice recorder and begin to prophesy over yourself. The words you speak can be a self-fulfilling prophecy. In Psalm 103, David tells his soul to bless the Lord, repeatedly. Speak to your heart, worship God and prophesy over yourself.

EXERCISE 7
Getting Words of Knowledge Using a Diving Board (group)
The person in the middle asks God for information about the person

in front of him by using a "diving board" statement. This can be saying things such as: "People have told you …", "You have said …", "Do you have pain in …?", "Is there someone here who …?", "When you were … years old …" After the "diving board" statement, let a word of knowledge flow. All information can be tested easily to see if the person has tapped into the prophetic flow of revelation, or if they are simply guessing.

One evening I was training a friend of mine in prophecy. She gets up every morning at 4:30 a.m. to pray and spends significant time with God daily. I gave her some diving boards and called some friends of mine. "Tell them what happened yesterday," or, "Tell them what they have said or what other people have said about them." Ninety percent of what she said to people was accurate. She had a strong prophetic gift but she needed a diving board like this to activate it.

CHAPTER 5

Teaching Children to Prophesy

> And he said: "Truly, I say to you, unless you turn and become like children, you will never enter the kingdom of heaven."
> – MATTHEW 18:3

> Before I formed you in the womb I knew you, and before you were born I consecrated you; I appointed you a prophet to the nations.
> – JEREMIAH 1:5

Prophecy isn't just for grown-ups. It is also for children. My sister-in-law, Esther, once went to the parent-teacher meeting to discuss the grades of her then nine-year-old daughter, Gracie. As she went into the classroom the teacher said, "Did you know your daughter Gracie is a prophet?"

The teacher, a widow, had lost her husband. He had been robbed and murdered. She was mourning and thinking, "My life has no color. My life is totally black and white. I have nothing but sadness, hurt and pain."

All the children were busy with coloring when little Gracie came up to the teacher's table. She asked her if she could show her something. It was a picture full of many colors. "Teacher, God says your life is full of many colors. He says you have so many special gifts and talents. Look, see the colors, every one of them represents gifts in your life."

Gracie proceeded to describe each color as something special her teacher had in her life. Her teacher was shocked. God used this little girl to speak to her through the picture she had colored, and that morning changed her life. She still has the picture and often talks about the little nine-year old blonde prophet in her classroom.

The Bible is full of examples of God using people from a young age. Jesus was twelve years old when He baffled the pharisees and teachers of the law in the temple with His knowledge (Luke 2:41-52). Samuel was just a young boy when God began speaking to him for the first time (1 Sam. 3:10-11). God told Jeremiah: "Do not say, 'I am only a youth'; for to all to whom I send you, you shall go, and whatever I command you, you shall speak" (Jer. 1:6-7). A young boy shared his lunch with Jesus so he could feed thousands of people (John 6:9).

The prophet Jeremiah says: " ... they shall all know me, from the least of them to the greatest, declares the LORD" (31:34). The Bible also states, "In the last days it shall be, God declares, that I will pour out my Spirit on all flesh, and your sons and your daughters shall prophesy, and your young men shall see visions, and your old men shall dream dreams ... and they shall prophesy" (Acts 2:17-18).

God speaks to children. Munday Martin describes how his three-year-old helped them avoid a potentially fatal car accident. One morning a friend of his told him, "Munday, listen to your children because God is going to speak to you through them." That evening as they were driving home his son said, "Mommy, I hit truck." Martin's wife told him to slow down and pull over into another lane. Thirty seconds later, they saw a truck had stopped right in the middle of the lane they had been driving in at 55 miles per hour. They would have rammed the truck if they had not heeded the words of their three-year old son.[23]

My favorite prophetic ministers are my own children. When we have family devotions, we will read the Bible, pray and ask God to speak to us through a picture. Sometimes, the things my children see are simply their own imaginations, but sometimes, they really are a word from God. One day I asked Hannah to ask Jesus for a picture for someone. Without knowing who it was, she said, "I see music notes and I believe God says He loves your music and wants you to make music." The person whom she had sent this to was just sitting at home with her guitar wondering whether or not she should start playing it again. When she got that word from Hannah, she knew God was answering her prayer. She is now my children's guitar teacher. That prophetic word had great musical fruit for her life and ours. At a church we once visited, my then seven-year-old son Levi told a woman, "I see donuts above your head." Everyone laughed, because she is in charge of hospitality and gets the donuts for the church meetings.

One person I trained in prophecy is a teacher at a Christian school. She asked her elementary students to ask Jesus to speak to them in a picture. Every one of them got a picture from Jesus. Prophesying is perfectly normal for children!

As we get older, many of us lose the freedom and creativity we had as children. Many of us basically draw in the same fashion as we drew when we were ten or twelve years old. Our creativity seems to stop around that age. We become more and more inhibited as we get older. This is part of the reason why Jesus said we must become like children to come into the kingdom of heaven (Matt. 18:3).

Often, prophets have child-like faith. One friend of mine told me, "If a wall is red, but God says it is blue, I believe God." This is the mustard seed-like faith God can use to move mountains. Another prophet starts crying like a child whenever he feels the presence of God. I call him the weeping prophet because he has such a sensitivity to and love of God's presence.

Throughout Church history there are accounts of moves of God which have involved children. During my senior year of high school, some of us students had been praying God would do something special that year. On 31 October, during chapel we had a visitation of the manifest presence of God. Pastor Billy Joe Daugherty recognized this and sent all of us high school students to go pray for the elementary students. That day had enormous impact. We had no class as students and teachers were being touched by the presence of God. I remember walking into the elementary classrooms and experiencing God's tangible presence. God visited us! Students fell under the power of God and burst into tears. We prayed like never before. Those of us who experienced it still talk about what took place that day.

Helping Children Grow

The best time to train people in following Christ is as children. Proverbs 22:6 says, "Train up a child in the way he should go; even when he is old he will not depart from it." If a child experiences God at a young age, they will never forget him.

I was eleven years old when I consciously met a prophet for the first time. He simply placed his hand on me and told me how much God loved me. Those simple words impacted me deeply. For the next forty-eight hours, I felt like I was in the palm of God's hand. I also began seeing more pictures when I would worship and pray. Callings, too, can be clear from a very young age. I remember traveling with my father as a child and watching him preach and pray for the sick. My biggest desire was to someday become like my father and do the things he did. I am now doing what my father did and teaching others to do the same.

Having said that, children should be allowed to be children. Do not force children to minister. Do not place the responsibility of large decisions on their shoulders. As adults we are responsible for cultivating the prophetic in our children while protecting them. At one church where I ministered with Hannah and Levi, Levi got bored and went to play video games while Hannah and I finished prophesying over the rest of the people.

Do encourage children and give them the opportunity to grow in prophetic ministry. Encourage them even when things they say may not be totally accurate or correct. Be a loving and encouraging mentor for them. You can help or hinder your children's growth in the prophetic.

I was twelve years old when I started prophesying at a house group. My father shut me down because he felt I was too young to prophesy. Even though we grew up in a church which believed in the gifts of the Holy Spirit and prophecy, it was still seen as mysterious and possibly even dangerous. Recently I found out why my father shut me down at that moment. He said my prophetic word was incorrect. I was prophesying amazing things over a man who was not nearly as good as I was describing him. My father was correct in stopping me at that moment and he definitely had the authority to do so. The unfortunate part was I did not have an opportunity to further develop this gift for years. God spoke to me, yet it was in 2010 I found out I could intentionally develop and grow in the prophetic ministry.

Helping children to prophesy is very simple. This is how I do it: my children and I close our eyes and ask Jesus to show us a picture. We share the picture we see and then we ask Jesus what the picture means. I am astounded by the pictures and the meaning my kids come up with at times.

One day Levi said, "I see trousers."

"Levi, what does Jesus want to say with that?" I asked.

"I think that just like trousers keep us safe and warm, so I think that Jesus says he wants to keep us safe and warm."

I was shocked by the simplicity and beauty of the message my son had just given me.

It is normal for parents I train to send me prophetic messages from their children. Often before they go to bed and do their time of prayer, they will make time to ask Jesus for a word or a picture. One girl, without knowing me at all, sent me a word saying God was going to use me all over the world. A six-year-old began prophesying over me and my entire family when her mom and dad started filming here. Her words were very simple, but also very strengthening, encouraging and comforting.

At one church in Nevada, I saw a twelve-year-old girl getting accurate words of knowledge and seeing many healings take place as she prayed for people. At Oradea, Romania, I saw a seven-year-old healing the sick and absolutely loving the prophetic conference. She said, "If Papa and Mama take me to Grandma's again the next time there's a prophetic conference, I will be very angry at them!" Children can really love God in a way we as adults can learn from.

My daughter grabs a microphone with great courage and begins to prophesy or pray for someone's healing. If God can use her, He can use anybody. Do not see children as nuisances

who need to be babysat while we do "real" church. They are
God's children who can also hear His voice. As an eighteen-
year-old, I wrote down part of my life's mission as being to
"raise up a new generation of worshipers ... who make known
the life, the power and voice of God to the world." In other
words: change the world, start with your children!

I titled this chapter "Teaching Children to Prophesy," but
children can teach us something about prophecy as well. Each
and every one of us needs to become like a child in order to
prophesy. We're often much too worried about prophesying.
God is our Daddy, and He loves to talk to His children. So,
what's stopping you from prophesying and teaching your
children?

If you long to grow in the prophetic as a family, you can
also use Jennifer Toledo's prophetic course *Eyes that See
and Ears that Hear*. In her book *Children and the Supernatural*,
Toledo shares many inspiring stories on how God works
through children.[24]

PROPHESY—*JUST DO IT!*

EXERCISE 1
Draw a Picture (family/group)

Have children (or adults) pray for someone and then ask Jesus for a
picture for them. Have them draw a picture and then explain what
they think Jesus wants to say to them. My son once drew a picture
of me riding on a horse as a knight killing a dragon. A week later a

friend of mine had a prophetic dream of me riding on a horse killing a dragon. I immediately sent him a copy of my son's picture. What an amazing confirmation!

EXERCISE 2
Send an Encouraging Word to Someone Not Present (individual/family/group)

Have your child say what they think Jesus wants to tell someone. Send this word to this person, for example via WhatsApp or Facebook. You can send it as a text or record it as a video or sound fragment. When possible, ask the receiver for feedback.

EXERCISE 3
Call Someone and Prophesy Over Each Other (individual/family)

One of my friends developed a fun prophetic exercise you can also practice with children. He calls a friend and asks, "So how am I doing?" Then the other person would ask God and begin to share what they felt, saw or heard.

EXERCISE 4
Ask God What May Happen This Week, Month(s), or Year (individual/family)

You can ask God for details of what may happen in the future. Write the things down. Then you can always check your journal to see if they come to pass. Though this may not always happen, it is encouraging to see when they do take place.

God regularly tells children what will happen. When a Cuban friend of mine was about eleven years old, God told him he'd go to the United States one month before his fourteenth birthday and he would travel through another country. This friend told his family – they didn't believe him. But sure enough, everything happened just as God had said.

Sometimes I call a friend and we ask God to share with us what the theme, goal, challenges and strategies will be for each of the three months that are coming. We write down what we see, and amazingly God has spoken to us in significant ways with this exercise.

EXERCISE 5

Wheel Inside of a Wheel (group)

Split the entire group into two different groups. Have one group make an interior circle and the rest of the other group surround them. The inner group will face the outer group and everyone in the inner group will prophesy over the other group. Have the people in the inside circle switch clockwise so they will have a new person to prophesy over. After a while, have the outer group persons then prophesy over the inner group.

This is a great exercise to get everyone prophesying and receiving prophetic words. Combine it with other exercises such as 'The Blind Prophet' (chapter 4 exercise 5) or 'Getting Words of Knowledge Using a Diving Board' (chapter 4 exercise 7) to change things up. I enjoy using this exercise at the end of prophetic evenings to be able to receive prophetic ministry and evaluate people's prophetic flow.

Creating a Healthy Prophetic Culture

There is plenty of teaching available on how to become a pastor, teacher and even an evangelist, but there is relatively little regarding the ministry of the prophet. Many people who feel such a calling on their lives do not know where they can go for this kind of help and mentoring. When I began, I found few resources which could aid the development of the ministry of the prophet. It is my prayer this book, among many others, becomes such a resource. I hope this will teach people to prophesy and raise up new prophets. We should do the same as Samuel, Elijah and Elisha: they all raised up schools of prophets in order to establish a new generation of prophets for their day. It is one of my great joys to see communities of prophets growing up and excelling in prophetic ministry. Since 2010 I have organized schools of prophecy around the world. I remember my first very well. I was amazed to see how large groups of people of all ages began boldly, accurately and scripturally prophesying. I have seen hundreds of people activated and growing in accurate and life-giving prophetic ministry.

Whenever I travel, I endeavor to take a team with me and identify budding prophets in different cities of the world. This is a deliberate and strategic way of mentoring a new generation of prophetic ministers and prophets. I also intentionally nurture and cultivate relationships with developing and seasoned prophets.

The best way to learn something is together with other people. Do you want to learn to prophesy? Find other people with whom you can grow in prophetic ministry. Practice and experiment regularly with the different activation exercises described in this book to become stronger in your gift. Do not feel obligated to do all of them, but experiment to see different ways God may speak to you.

Church leaders can promote a culture in which prophecy is normal and common. A lot of churches rely too heavily on their pastors. Pastors do all ministry work and regular Christians just watch them do it. Not only is it unhealthy, it is unbiblical. Paul speaks of a five-fold ministry team of apostles, prophets, evangelists, pastors and teachers (Eph. 4:11-13). Activating people and having them join in is essential for creating a strong and healthy church. My greatest success is not when *I* prophesy, preach, teach, pastor or heal the sick, but when I get to see those I have trained prophesying, preaching, teaching, pastoring or healing the sick. What steps can you as a leader take to create a healthy prophetic culture in your church?

1. Ensure people understand the difference between prophecy in the Old Testament and New Testament. This is where people are full of grace and truth and not just the law (John 1:17). Be leaders and be prophets who are full of love, humility, generosity and courage.

2. Create a culture where everyone gets to play. Use the exercises described in this book to activate the prophetic in your life and in the lives of people in your church. If this is all totally new for you, seek out strong prophets who have more experience in the prophetic and learn from them.

3. Create safe places where people can prophesy and receive prophetic ministry. This may be a prophetic evening once or twice a month dedicated to prophetic ministry. Or you can set up prophetic ministry teams who can prophesy over people before, during or after church services. Train your entire church to prophesy, not just "special" people.

4. Encourage people to prophesy outside of the church in the course of their regular daily lives. Prophetic ministry is not just for the church, but for all areas of life. God loves to speak to people at supermarkets or on the streets.

5. Teach others everything you know and you will come to know much more. This is why I love to teach, demonstrate and activate people in the prophetic myself.

Create communities or "schools" of prophets and prophetic ministers. Just like fish swim together, Christians can "swim" in the spirit of prophesy together. "Two are better than one" and a team is better than two (see Eccles. 4:9).

6. Social media sites are good channels to learn about prophecy and keep in touch with other prophets. I use WhatsApp, Facebook groups and Zoom to mentor and train leaders throughout the world in prophetic ministry.

7. Read good books about this topic. You will grow more confident and learn about prophecy. You'll avoid making some mistakes. It's great to learn from your own mistakes, but even better to learn from other people's mistakes! (In the section Recommended Reading, you'll find titles I found helpful.

In 2010, my world was radically rocked by a prophet who told me, "Everything I can do, you can do better. Just do it." Since then, I tell people who want to grow in prophecy: "Just do it."

Do you know the story of Elijah? He left his prophet mantle to Elisha, who did twice as many miracles as Elijah. With this book I leave my prophet mantle to you. I pray that everyone picking up this mantle will experience all that I have experienced with God and so much more! That's my desire for my children, but also for my readers and the people I teach. So, do you want to grow in hearing God's voice and speaking His words? Do you want to prophesy?

JUST DO IT!

Notes

THE VISION

1. Foster, R. (2008). *Prayer: Finding the Heart's True Home.* London: Hodder & Stoughton, 261.
2. Foster, 262.

CHAPTER 1

3. facebook.com/caminodevida.bolivia (accessed December 10, 2018).

CHAPTER 2

4. Bruce Foster taught this in May 2016 at our church in Amsterdam.
5. Quoted in Keller, T. *Humility.* Sermon at gospelinlife.com/humility-6125 (accessed December 10, 2018).
6. Nearly every question about speaking in tongues and the baptism in the Holy Spirit is answered in Basham, D. (1969). *Ministering the Baptism in the Holy Spirit.* New Kensington, PA: Whitaker House.
7. vineyardchurches.org.uk/articles/how-thevineyard-began (accessed 3 October 2018).
8. Eckhardt, J. (2009). *God Still Speaks.* Lake Mary, FL: Charisma House, 10.
9. Hagin, K. (2006). *How You Can Be Led by the Spirit of God.* Tulsa, OK: Faith Library Publications, 119.
10. Wimber, J. in Wimber, J. & Springer, K. (2009). *Power Evangelism.* Grand Rapids, MI: Chosen Books, 7.

CHAPTER 3

11. Putman, P. (2013). *School of Kingdom Ministry Manual.* Oklahoma City, OK: Coaching Saints Publications, 10.
12. Vallotton, K. (2015). *School of the Prophets.* Bloomington: Chosen Books, 77.
13. Hagin, 120.
14. Tucker, C. (2004). *In Search of Purpose ... En Route to Destiny.* Tulsa, OK: Polished Arrows International, 47.
15. thequietstreet.wordpress.com/2012/07/22/if-the-spirits-not-moving-will-move-him/ (accessed December 13, 2018).
16. Hagin, 75.
17. Vallotton, K. (2005, expanded edition 2014). *Basic Training For The Prophetic Ministry.* Shippensburg: Destiny Image, 34.

CHAPTER 4

18. Bickle, M. (1995). *Growing in the Prophetic.* Eastbourne: Kingsway Publications, 183-191.
19. Bolz, S. (2015). *Translating God.* Glendale, CA: ICreate Productions.
20. Iglesia Crusaders (2004). *School of the Prophets,* 17.
21. Hagin, 114.
22. Cooke, G. (1994). *Developing Your Prophetic Gifting.* Tonbridge ,Kent: Sovereign World Ltd., 199-201. I discovered this in Harrisson, D. (2013). *The Power of Prophetic Teams.* Belleville, ON: Essence Publishing, Kindle Locations 199-202.

CHAPTER 5

23. godencounters.com/youth-awakening-worldwide-revival-among-children/ (accessed August 13, 2018).
24. Toledo, J. (2007). *Eyes that See and Ears that Hear.* Dinuba: Global Children's Movement, and Toledo, J. (2012). *Children and the Supernatural.* Lake Mary: Charisma House.

Recommended Reading

Bolz, S. (2015). *Translating God*. Glendale, CA: ICreate Productions.

Bolz, S. (2017). *God Secrets*. Glendale, CA: ICreate Productions.

Bolz, S. (2018). *Modern Prophets*. Glendale, CA: ICreate Productions.

Campbell, W. & S. (2016). *Praying the Bible*. Grand Rapids, MI: Chosen Books.

Clement, K. (2005). *Secrets of the Prophetic*. Shippensburg, PA: Destiny Image.

Cooke, G. (2000). *Developing Your Prophetic Gifting*. Lancaster: Sovereign World Ltd.

Cooke, G. (2006). *Approaching the Heart of Prophecy*. Vacaville, CA: Brilliant Book House.

Cooke, G. (2009). *Prophecy and Responsibility*. Vacaville, CA: Brilliant Book House.

Cooke, G. (2010). *Prophetic Wisdom*. Vacaville, CA: Brilliant Book House.

Dedmon, K. (2007). *The Ultimate Treasure Hunt*. Shippensburg, PA: Destiny Image.

Eckhardt, J. (2017). *The Prophet's Manual*. Lake Mary, FL: Charisma House.

Foster, R.J. (2001) *Streams of Living Water*. New York: HarperOne

Foster, R.J. (2008). *Prayer*. London: Hodder & Stoughton.

Goll, J.W. (2012). *The Seer*. Shippensburg, PA: Destiny Image.

Hagin, K.E. (2006). *How You Can Be Led by the Spirit of God*. Tulsa, OK: Faith Library Publications.

Harrison, D. (2017). *The Power of Prophetic Teams*. CreateSpace Independent Publishing Platform.

Jersak, B. (2003). *Children, Can You Hear Me?*. Abbotsford: Fresh Wind Press.

Toledo, J. (2007). *Eyes that See and Ears that Hear*. Dinuba: Global Children's Movement

Toledo, J. (2012). *Children and the Supernatural*. Lake Mary: Charisma House.

Vallotton, K. (2005, expanded edition 2014). *Basic Training For The Prophetic Ministry*. Shippensburg: Destiny Image.

Vallotton, K. (2015). *School of the Prophets*. Bloomington: Chosen Books.

Willard, D. (2012). *Hearing God*. Downers Grove, IL: IVP Books.

Warner, L. (2010). *Journey with Jesus*. Downers Grove, IL: IVP Books.

Wimber, J. & Springer, K. (2009). *Power Evangelism*. Grand Rapids, MI: Chosen Books.

Matthew Helland

Born in Chile to American missionaries, Matthew Helland is an international missionary, speaker and writer. He is based out of Amsterdam, the Netherlands. In the past few years his ministry has taken him to nations throughout Europe, North America, South America, the Middle East and to Australia. He is fluent in English, Dutch and Spanish.

Matthew feels called to activate churches in evangelism and the gifts of the Spirit. He frequently teaches on subjects such as:

- discipleship
- prophecy
- power evangelism
- divine healing
- prayer
- church planting

Matthew and his wife Femke live in Amsterdam with their four children. After planting a church there, they are now focusing on reaching out to Spanish speaking individuals in the city's Red-Light District. There, they are seeing lives transformed by the love of God and the power of the Holy Spirit!

newlife equip

www.newlifeequip.org
www.prophesyandheal.com
www.facebook.com/mattandfemke.helland

ARROWZ

Cutting-edge Materials
for Radical Followers of Christ

For questions and bulk discount orders
please contact us at info@arrowz.org